SCOTTISH DANCE

HarperCollins Publishers
Westerhill Road
Bishopbriggs
Glasgow
G64 2QT

First Edition 2017

Reprint 10 9 8 7 6 5 4 3 2 1 0

© HarperCollins Publishers 2017

ISBN 978-0-00-821056-4

Collins® is a registered
trademark of HarperCollins
Publishers Limited

www.collins.co.uk

A catalogue record for this
book is available from the
British Library

Compiled in association with The Royal
Scottish
Edited b[...]
and Will[...]

Typeset
Davidso[...]

Printed
RR Don[...]

HarperCollins does not
warrant that www.collins.co.uk
or any other website mentioned
in this title will be provided

Contents

Introduction

What are Scottish Dance, Scottish Country Dance, and Ceilidh Dancing?

Scottish dance refers to the types of dances that have been danced socially in Scotland over many years. For the purposes of this book a good starting point is to take a quick look at the state of social dance in Scotland in the early 20th century. Before the First World War the social pattern of dancing included a variety of dances that covered different traditional styles. However, by the end of the war traditional dances were being challenged in many areas by ballroom dances and dances influenced by syncopated rhythms. Traditional dancing in Scotland was under threat in many areas, particularly the set dances, as couple dancing started to dominate.

Today the two main types of dancing that are done socially, and can also be considered to be Scottish, are Scottish country dancing and Scottish ceilidh dancing. Although they are sometimes considered to be completely separate they have much in common and are bound together by the music and some shared dances.

Country dancing is, historically, a form of dance performed by groups of couples, called sets, usually consisting of three or more couples adjacent to each other in two parallel lines, the men facing the women. An important feature of the country dance is that it is usually progressive. After each turn of the dance, the couple at the top, who begin the dance, finish one place further down, then each of the other couples in succession, having reached the top, take their turn as leading couple.

Although it is the case that most country dances are danced in longwise sets, other dance styles have been incorporated into the country dance repertoire: for example, square set formation and two-couple dances, where the dancers move progressively round the dance floor.

A further feature of Scottish country dancing is that, although there are many simple dances that can be danced easily by the novice dancer, there are also a significant number of more complex dances that require some degree of proficiency by the participants. Scottish country dancing can either be very informal or be presented in a formal manner, with regard to both style and dress.

A typical Scottish country dance consists of a series of well-known formations which are arranged in a different sequence for each dance, hence, having mastered the basic steps and formations, a Scottish country dancer should be able to participate happily and easily wherever there is country dancing.

Ceilidh dancing is a dance form that has derived from the Old Time dances and couple dances that found their way onto the Scottish dance floor in the 19th century. It also includes some simple country dances that have generally been part of the Scottish repertoire for many years. In some ways ceilidh dancing has derived directly from the old village hall dances in the more rural parts of Scotland and has been largely untouched by any formal attempt to standardise its execution and formations. In some rural communities what would be called a ceilidh dance in Glasgow or Edinburgh would just be a dance. Ceilidh dance is also defined by its accessibility, with just about anyone being able to get up and join in with minimal instruction. To aid in this, many ceilidhs today would be run by a caller who selects the dances to be done and provides basic instruction to ensure that the evening can be enjoyed by everyone.

This description of ceilidh dancing and Scottish country dancing might appear to be describing two completely separate dance forms. However, in reality they are both part of a Scottish dance spectrum – the very informal easily accessible dances at one end and the formal complex dances requiring some experience and technique at the other end. There are many clubs and events that occupy a position somewhere between these two extremes, where either informal Scottish country dancing is practised or Old Time and Scottish country dancing exist side by side. They are all danced to Scotland's amazing music and are great exercise: find out what suits you and seek out a club. You do not need to go with a partner – someone will always ask you to dance. Give it a go, it's very sociable, you'll get fit, have more fun than going to a gym, and make friends.

Short history of Scottish Dancing

Early references

Traditional dance is common to all cultures and in this respect Scotland is no different. References to dancing in Scotland go far back in Scottish history with both intrinsic native influences and ideas imported from other cultures. Variations have emerged in dance content, style, and musical inspiration.

Some of the earliest detailed written references to traditional dance in Scotland date back to the 17th century, when the main dance of the time was the 'reel', which is generally recognised as one of the truly indigenous dances of Scotland. This is a dance where the dancers alternated between steps that were danced on the spot and everyone dancing round in a circle or in a figure of eight. This type of dance gave its name to reels, both as a musical rhythm and as a dance form. There are references to highland reels being the commonest and preferred dance in many parts of Scotland even in the late 1800s. This was particularly so in the more remote locations of the Western Isles, Orkney, and Shetland.

Other dance forms were introduced into Scotland from the early 1700s and country dancing became popular in the dance assemblies in the cities, particularly in Edinburgh. Country dancing in this era was one of the most popular dance forms throughout Scotland, but the older 'reels' continued to be danced alongside the country dances.

The history of country dancing in Britain is complicated with some uncertainties regarding its origins. John Playford in London was the first person to write down country dance instructions along with their associated tunes in his first edition of the English Dancing Master, which was published in 1651. Some of Playford's early editions included dances with Scottish titles or tunes with Scottish titles. As there had been no Scottish publications of either traditional music or dance at this time it is unclear as to the exact origins of these early dances – all we know is that John Playford was the first person to publish country dances. We do know that as country dancing became more and more popular in Scotland, the influences from older dance forms, such as Scotch reels, became incorporated into country dances. In many ways these Scottish-influenced country dances could be considered the first genuinely Scottish country dances. By the middle of the 18th century various dancing masters were publishing collections of country dances specifically entitled Caledonian Country Dances.

Nineteenth-Century Developments

The years immediately following the end of the Napoleonic Wars in 1815 witnessed the spread of two new forms of dance, the quadrille and the waltz. The quadrille originated in France and incorporated four couples arranged in a square formation, with the dancers performing a series of sequences or formations, either with their opposite couples or with all four couples working together. As quadrilles developed in Britain, formations from quadrilles appeared in 19th-century country dances and vice versa. The waltz was the first of the couple dances to appear and become popular, but later in the 19th century other couple dances began to be introduced, such as the polka. These dances are often referred to as Old Time Dances or Sequence Dances. Some of these early couple dances are still being danced today and, along with some country dances from this period, form the basis of what has today become known as ceilidh dancing. Some popular 19th-century dances combined elements from different dance forms. The Waltz Country Dance, as its title implies, is a country dance in waltz tempo. The Glasgow Highlanders (the only strathspey popular in late-19th century ballroom) combines elements of the country dance with elements of the foursome reel. The universally known Eightsome Reel places a quadrille chorus around a series of threesome reel patterns.

Towards the end of the 19th century it would have been common for many dance events throughout Scotland to include dances from all of the styles that were round at that time, including Scotch reels, country dances, quadrilles and couple dances. Different parts of the country seemed to have different preferences for their dance repertoire but all styles of dances seemed to exist side by side in equal measure.

In many ways the late 19th century was probably both an exciting and a confusing time for Scottish social dancing. Some people worried about the decline of certain dance forms, and, at the same time, new dances were being developed which drew inspiration from the newer dance styles and also incorporated elements of older dances.

However, by the time of the First World War this pattern of social dance was being challenged by more modern influences, such as ballroom dances and other dances inspired by syncopated rhythms. Traditional social dancing as it had been practised and developed over many years was disappearing rapidly. In some ways the decline of the reels and country dances was less marked in Scotland than in other parts of Europe during this period. One reason for this was the system of dancing classes and schools which permeated Scottish society. Scottish dancing masters taught a wide repertoire, including quadrilles, reels, waltzes, polkas, solo dances, circle dances, and country dances. Dances like Petronella, Flowers of Edinburgh, and Duke of Perth were taught widely and were included in all the pocket manuals of dancing. A number of these manuals classify country dances as either 'English' or 'Scotch', partly on the basis of their tunes and their figures. Many thousands of copies of these manuals were sold; their instructions regarding polite behaviour, as well as dancing, appealed particularly to those who wished to rise in the world.

Other reasons for the survival of social dancing in Scotland were the tradition of dancing in the Scottish regiments (where dancing was an obligatory activity) and the comparative lack of social division in Scotland. The traditional dances were supported by the nobility and gentry, with lairds in many rural areas giving annual balls for their tenants. Such evenings of social dancing were occasions when all levels of society came together to enjoy the pleasures of the traditional Scottish dances and music.

There has also been a long history of Scottish Balls, where the nobility and gentry danced. The Perth Ball originally dates from 1820 and has been taking place virtually every year since. This has provided continuity for some country dances and reels over a long time period. The first Royal Caledonian Ball in London took place in the 1840s and again has a long, uninterrupted history, apart from when the country has been at war.

However, outside of the Caledonian Ball circuit, social dance was changing rapidly, and in the years immediately following the First World War, Scottish dance faced an uncertain future. The majority of Scots now lived in large towns and cities and young people flocked to commercial ballrooms, where they danced the foxtrot and other dances inspired by new syncopated rhythms. Traditional social dances almost disappeared. Thanks to the work of the Scottish Country Dance Society (SCDS), however, the Scottish country dance survived and gained worldwide popularity. The revival of strathspey country dances, with many fine tunes both traditional and newly composed to accompany them, is entirely due to the work of the SCDS.

Traditional Dance Revival
The early decades of the 20th century saw a revival of interest in traditional dance and song in England. The English Folk Dance Society (EFDS), founded in 1911 by Cecil Sharp, published several books of English country dances. In 1912 the Beltane Society was formed in Glasgow with similar aims: 'to cultivate among the younger generation knowledge of Scottish folk songs, ballads, dances, and singing games'. At a festival held by the Beltane Society in Glasgow in 1912, Blue Bonnets, Flowers of Edinburgh, and The Nut were included in the

programme. Miss Jean Milligan of Jordanhill College, Glasgow also began to include the Scottish dances in her work as a lecturer in Physical Training for student teachers. The Beltane Society, however, did not survive the outbreak of the First World War.

Cecil Sharp's books were enthusiastically adopted by the recently formed Girl Guides Association and the dances they contained were taught to Guides in Scotland as well as in England. Mrs Ysobel Stewart of Fasnacloich, Guide Commissioner for Argyll, believed that Girl Guides in Scotland should learn Scottish country dances. To make that possible, a book similar to those available from the EFDS was required. Mrs Stewart, therefore, wrote out in a notebook the Scottish dances which she remembered from the Highland balls of her youth, including the music to accompany them. She approached Michael Diack of the Glasgow publishers Paterson's, who agreed to publish the dances, provided their correctness was verified. He arranged for Mrs Stewart to meet Miss Milligan. From this meeting, in the autumn of 1923, grew the plan to publish a book of twelve Scottish country dances and also to form a

Society to support the new publication. The Scottish Country Dance Society (SCDS) was formed at a public meeting held in Glasgow on the 26th November 1923 and attended by twenty-seven interested people. The partnership of Mrs Stewart and Miss Milligan provided the Society with a firm foundation on which to grow and develop. The first book of dances was published in 1924 and since then the Society has continued to publish books of dances, organise teaching activities, and provide other services to the Scottish country dance community. The title 'Royal' was conferred upon the Society by King George VI in 1951. Queen Elizabeth II, as HRH Princess Elizabeth, became Patron of the Society in 1946 and continues as Patron today.

The RSCDS, now a Scottish Charity, has been so successful since its formation in 1923 that there are now RSCDS branches and other affiliated Scottish country dance groups throughout the world. So wherever you live there is a good chance that there will a group of Scottish dancers nearby who are sure to give you a warm welcome.

Terms and definitions

The intention for this book is to keep the instructions for the dances as simple as possible, so that they can be understood easily. It is inevitable, however, that there are a number of key words that will be used in the dance instructions that the 'new dancer' may find confusing at first. This chapter explains the meanings of these words and expressions so that when you meet them in the instructions they should be more easily understood.

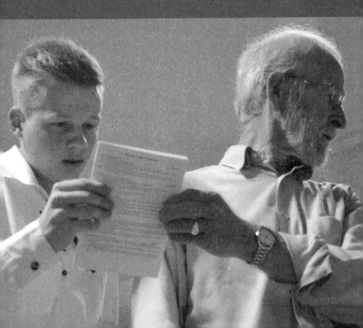

This chapter is split into three sections:

Section 1   Describes a number of terms that are frequently encountered when dancing ceilidh or country dancing. They cover things such as basic direction, steps and holds, etc.

Section 2   Covers the starting positions for the various dance types included in the book, the type and shape of country dance sets, and the type of progression to be found in country dances.

Section 3   Describes some of the formations that occur in the country dances.

Some of these descriptions may seem a bit daunting, requiring a degree of knowledge and technical skill, but please don't be put off. Rules for dancing are used as a guide to help people dance together, so that the dance works for all taking part. They should not be considered prescriptive but are there to help create the framework for the dance.

You might in some circumstances find that there are some strange etiquette procedures that dancers follow when dancing Scottish dances. Good manners should, of course, be a natural part of dancing with others and some conventions have developed over the years. It is polite to wait until a dance is announced before making up sets. Dancers should join sets at the end of a line rather than in the middle of sets that are possibly already made up. Above all, when dancing be aware of others on the dance floor, so that we all engage with and help each other through the dance.

1. General Terms

Key to figures
In the figures in Sections 3, 4, and 5, men are represented by green cirles ⬤ and women by blue squares ▪.

The numbers in the circles and squares indicate the positions of each dancer. 1 is the leading couple.

⬤ ▪ — shows starting position

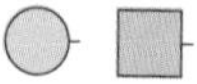

⬤ ▪ — shows direction in which the dancers are facing

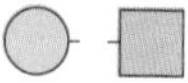

⬤ ▪ — shows dancers facing each other

⌢ — indicates direction of travel

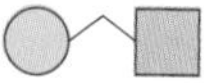

⬤⬠▪ — indicates hands are joined

Line of Dance
This is used to describe the direction of travel of the dancers round the dance floor. For all the round-the-room type dances described in this book, the line of dance is in an anticlockwise direction round the dance floor. The term only applies to couple dances, not to set dances.

Against the line of dance
Opposite to line of dance – that is, clockwise direction round the dance floor.

Top/Bottom
The end of the dance floor nearest the band or music is referred to as the top, with the part of the dance floor furthest from the band being the bottom. These terms are only relevant to set dances (longwise or square), the couple nearest the music in each set being the top or 1st couple. Dancing towards the top of the set is called dancing up and dancing away from the top of the set is called dancing down.

Opposite
In a longwise set the dancers stand opposite their partners. If a dancer finishes a movement or formation on their partner's side of the set, they are on the opposite side.

Opposite is also used in sets of two couples, where one couple faces another, when dancing with a dancer from the other couple.

Ballroom Hold

Couples face each other: the man places his right hand round his partner's waist while she places her left hand on his right shoulder. They join their other hands at shoulder height, almost at arm's length.

Open Hold

Couples stand side by side, the man with his partner on his right and with nearer hands joined.

Promenade Hold

Couples face in the same direction, men with their partner on their right, and join both hands, left in left, right in right, with the right hands above left hands. The arms are held away from the body, comfortably above waist height.

Allemande Hold

This hold is used when dancing an allemande and also the Gay Gordons. Couples face in the same direction, men with their partner on their right, and join both hands, left in left, right in right, with the right above left. The man raises the woman's right hand over her head to hold it just above, but not resting on, her right shoulder. The left hands and arms are held away from the body, comfortably above waist height.

Waltz turn
Many of the couple dances complete the turn through the dance with a four-bar waltz turn or rotary waltz turn. The couples take ballroom hold and dance a waltz, rotating clockwise, and at the same time moving slightly forward along the line of dance.

This terminology is also used in many dances that are not done in waltz tempo but in 6/8 or 4/4 march tempo. The instructions are the same.

This turn is also used as a progression in the dance 'Waltz Country Dance'.

Petronella turn
This is the name given to a two-bar turning movement on the diagonal. The name is taken from the dance Petronella, where the movement first occurred. The formation can be danced from the sidelines into the middle of the set, or from the middle of the set into the sidelines. It may be preceded by or followed by setting. It is danced turning to the right.

The dancing couple each dance diagonally to the right, dance a three-quarter turn, rotating clockwise, to finish facing their partner, either up and down the set or across the set, depending on the starting position. For example, when the turn is started from the sidelines, the dancers end up facing each other up and down the set.

One petronella turn takes two bars of music.

Top   Bottom

Dance Steps

There are many ways to do the dances in this book, from using formal dance steps all the way through to using walking steps. All are fine, what is most important is that you enjoy the dances and do your best to keep in time with the music.

Bars and counts

One of the most important aspects of dancing Scottish dances is to know where you are in the dance, how long each movement or formation takes, and what happens next. All the instructions in this book are broken down into bars of music, with the directions for each formation being related to the musical phrases expressed in bars. If you are not used to the music this may seem a bit daunting, but each phrase of the music is usually fairly easy to identify. The music for all Scottish dances is made up of eight-bar phrases. Everyone finds it easy to march or walk to a Scottish tune and for this book each natural walking beat is termed a count. Depending on the dance and the type of tune being used, the number of counts per bar of music can vary. So for each dance the counts per bar has been stated.

Travelling steps

The most basic travelling step is to walk rhythmically in time to the music. One step would take one beat or count. The number of counts in each bar of the music is given at the start of each dance instruction.

Country dancers use skip change of step for travelling, which is done as follows:

1   Hop on the left foot and at the same time bring the right foot forward
2   Step onto the right foot
3   Close the left foot behind the right foot
4   Step onto the right foot again.

This is one step and occupies one bar of music in reel or jig time. To continue travelling the step is repeated with the left foot. When done well, this is a very fluid step.

An alternative to the skip change of step is to skip. When skipping there are two skips for each bar of jig or reel time music.

The travelling step in strathspey time is very similar to the skip change of step with the exception that there is no hop or skip at the start.

Setting
Setting is a means of dancing on the spot. In some of the Old Time couple dances, the term 'balance' is used to describe a gentle setting step. For most of these dances you will find that you don't set on your own but facing another dancer, usually your partner. In Scottish country dancing the setting step used is the pas de basque, and a basic description is:

1 Step to the right
2 Bring the left foot to the right foot and transfer weight onto the left foot and bring the right foot off the floor
3 Transfer weight back to the right foot and
4 Extend the left foot forwards and to the left.

This is then repeated, starting to the left.

The whole of this sequence setting first on the right foot and then on the left is one setting step and takes two bars of music.

Strathspey setting
A different setting step is used in strathspey time.

1 Take a step to the right
2 Bring the left foot towards the right and close such that the two feet touch (left instep into right heel)
3 Take another step to the right
4 Bring the left foot up to the side of the right leg and hop.

Repeat this back in the other direction starting with the left foot.

The whole of this sequence setting first on the right foot and then on the left is one setting step and takes two bars of music.

Slip step
This step is used to travel sideways in formations such as circles or when dancing sideways with partner and with both hands joined. Two slip steps take one bar of music. The step described below is for moving to the left.

1 Take a step to the left with the left foot
2 Close the right foot to the left foot with heels touching.

Repeat as required. The above sequence occupies half a bar of music.

Chasse

The chasse step is done frequently in many of the couple dances. It is a simple side step and is described below for the man with his back to the centre of the room; left shoulder pointing along the line of dance.

1　Take a step to the left
2　Close right
3　Step to the left
4　Close right

Repeat back, starting with the right foot.

The whole of the above is one chasse and takes four bars of music in waltz time and two bars in 6/8 or 4/4 march tempo. The movement is usually danced with the couple in ballroom hold or with both hands joined. The woman also moving along the line of dance, starting with the right foot.

2. Starting positions for dances

The dances described cover a range of styles and shapes; in some dances the dancers dance only with their partners, while in others the dancers are in sets of up to four or, in a few instances, more couples. This section covers some basic information that describes the basic starting positions.

Couple Dances
In most couple dances, the couples progress anticlockwise round the room, along the line of dance. There are two basic starting positions:

Couples Facing Line of Dance
The couples stand side by side, both facing the line of dance in open hold, with nearer hands joined, men with partner on their right. For some dances the couples may hold each other round the waist.

The dance is repeated until the music is finished.

Some dances of this type can be danced in a progressive manner, where one of the dancers moves on at a specific point in the dance to meet a new partner. The MC or Caller will indicate if the dance is to be progressive and when and how the progression takes place.

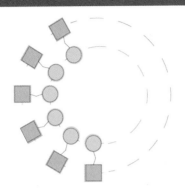

Couples in Line of Dance

The couples face each other in ballroom hold, men with their backs to the centre of the room and left shoulder facing line of dance.

The dance is repeated until the music is finished.

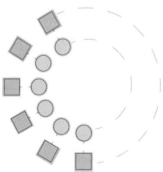

Circle Dance

Couples form a large circle, men with their partners on their right.

These dances are frequently progressive, with the dancers dancing with a new partner for every turn through the dance.

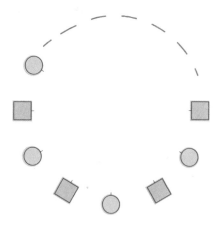

Round-the-room dance

Couples facing couples round the room, men with their partners on their right.

One of the couples faces clockwise round the dance floor and the other faces anticlockwise. The last formation of the dance is a progression, with each couple moving on past each other to meet a new couple.

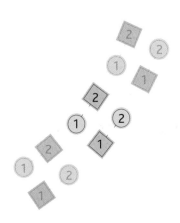

Longwise set dances

Sets of four (or more) couples in longwise formation, men with left shoulder to top of room, women on opposite side of the set facing partner.

Longwise

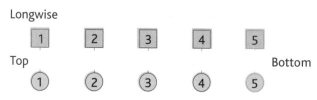

The first couple is the couple nearest the top of the room.

In a longwise set, each couple has the opportunity to dance as the leading or dancing couple, beginning from top place.

The simplest type of progression is where the top couple finish at the bottom of the set after one turn through the dance, with the second couple becoming the new top couple. The dance is repeated until all couples have completed their turn as top couple.

However, one of the commonest types of country dance progressions is where there are four couples in the set but the formations of the dance only involves three couples. After one turn through the dance, the top couple finish in second place and repeat the dance with the bottom two couples (the original second couple standing at the top of the set). After this second turn the top couple finish in third place, from where they move to the bottom of the set, changing places with the fourth couple. The second couple now begin their turn as top couple. After eight turns through the dance the couples should be back in their original positions.

1   After one turn through the dance the top couple finish in second place. First couple repeat the dance, dancing with third and fourth couples.

   End of 1st turn

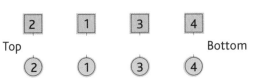

Top   Bottom

2 After the second turn through the dance, the top couple finish in third place.

End of 2nd turn

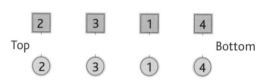

3 The original first couple step to the bottom of the set, as the fourth couple step up and the original second couple become the top couple. The dance is then repeated with second couple as top couple.

1st couple move to bottom
New top couple start

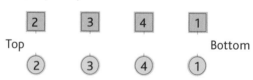

Some of the dances in this book are two-couple dances, where the dancing couple dance with the couple immediately below them. These dances are danced in four-couple sets and each couple dances the dance three times through before they get to the bottom of the set.

1   In the first turn through the dance, the first couple dance with the second couple and finish in second place.
2   For the second turn through the dance, the first couple dance with the third couple and finish the dance in third place.
3   For the third turn through the dance, the first couple dance with the fourth couple, finishing in fourth place, while the second couple start as the new top couple and dance with the third couple (now in second place) and finish in second place.
4   This pattern is continued until after eight turns through the dance the first couple is back in top place and all couples have completed their turns as top couple.

Square set dances

Four couples in a square set, men with their partners on their right.

The couple with their backs to the music are first couple, and couples are numbered clockwise round the set, so the couple on the left of first couple is second couple, the opposite couple is third couple, and the couple on the right fourth couple. The first and third couples are sometimes referred to as 'head' couples, with the second and fourth couples being 'side' couples.

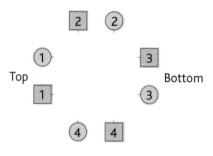

3. Formations

Allemande
An allemande is a form of progression.

It is usually danced with two couples, but can be adapted for three or four couples. It takes eight bars of music. Dancers start in the middle of the set, men with partners on their right, facing the top. To begin, the man takes his partner's right hand in his right and her left hand in his left. The man lifts his partner's right hand over her head to hold it just above shoulder height (see pic). This is called allemande hold.

Bars

1 – 4   In allemande hold, first couple, followed by second couple, dance a small step to the right, across the top of the set, and down the men's side. All finish facing down, in the order two, one (see fig).

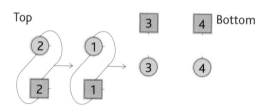

5   Each man brings his partner round into a line, all facing the women's side.

6   All dance into the middle, each man brings his partner round, under her right arm, to face him.

7 – 8   Releasing hands, all dance backwards to own sides.

Cast off or up

Casting is a form of progression.

To cast off one place, the dancers turn to the top of the set, face out, and dance down behind the next couple to finish one place down, facing each other across the set. This usually takes two bars of music but can be adapted to take four bars.

To cast up one place the dancers turn to the bottom of the set, face out, and dance up behind the next couple to finish one place up, facing each other across the set. This usually takes two bars of music but can be adapted to take four bars.

Dancers can also cast off or up, dancing behind two, three, or more couples.

Grand Chain

A grand chain is a formation with no progression.

It usually takes eight bars of music (sixteen walking steps) but can take sixteen bars (thirty-two walking steps). Dancers face alternately clockwise and anticlockwise and continue to dance in the same direction, giving right hands, then left hands, until the completion of the formation.

A grand chain for three couples usually begins with the couple at the top facing each other across the set, the couple in second place facing down, and the couple in third place facing up, giving right hands to begin.

A grand chain for four couples usually begins with first and fourth couples facing each other cross the set, second couple facing down and third couple facing up, giving right hands to begin.

In a square set all face partners and give right hands to begin.

Circle

A circle is a formation with no progression. It usually takes eight bars of music (sixteen walking steps). The circular formation of three, four, six, eight, or more dancers is maintained until the dancers return to the sidelines.

In reel and jig time, the dancers face the middle of the set and, using eight slip steps, move to the left, bring the heels together, change direction, and use eight slip steps to return to place.

In strathspey time, the dancers face the middle of the set and, using four travelling steps, move to the left, change direction, and use four travelling steps to return to place.

In many dance instructions, this formation is called 'hands round and back' with the number of hands indicating the number of dancers.

Corner formations

Longwise Sets

There are many formations with corner dancers and these need three couples. To identify corners, first couple begin back to back in the middle of the set, in second place, facing opposite sides. First corners are on the right of the first couple and second corners are on the left. That is, first woman's first corner is second man and her second corner is third man. Similarly, first man's first corner is third woman and his second corner is second woman (see fig).

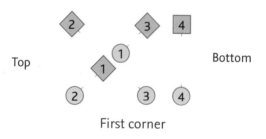

Top

Bottom

First corner

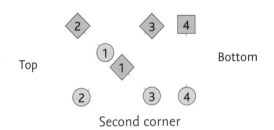

Top   Bottom

Second corner

Note: Corner positions remain fixed, but the
         corner dancers may change position
         during a formation or during the dance.

         Frequently the terms third and fourth
         corners are used. Third corner position
         being partner's first corner position and
         fourth corner position being partner's
         second corner position.

In Square Sets

In square sets the men have their partners on their right, the dancer on the left is their corner. Similarly, the women have their partners on their left and the dancer on the right is their corner.

Turn corners and partner

Turn corners and partner is a formation with no progression. It takes eight bars of music (sixteen walking steps). To begin, first couple are back to back in the middle of the set, facing first corners, in a diagonal line. Second couple are in top place.

Bars

1 – 2   First couple, giving right hands, turn first corners once round.

3 – 4   First couple, giving left hands, turn each other to face second corners.

5 – 6   First couple, giving right hands, turn second corners once round.

7 – 8   First couple, giving left hands, cross to own side of the dance to finish in second place.

Set to corners and turn
Three couples.

Eight bars of music (sixteen walking steps).

To begin, first couple are back to back in the middle of the set, facing first corners, in a diagonal line. Second couple are in top place.

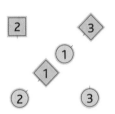

Bars

1 – 4   First couple and their first corners set to each other and turn with two hands, to finish with first couple back to back facing second corner.

5 – 8   First couple and their second corners set to each other and turn with two hands. The first couple finish in second position on the opposite side.

Back to back or do-si-do

Back to back is a four-bar (eight walking steps) formation danced by two individual dancers facing each other.

Bars

1 – 2   Dance forward, starting with the right foot, just passing partner by the right. The two dancers move slightly to their right to pass each other 'back to back'.

3 – 4   Dance backwards, passing partner by the left, to finish in original places.

Lead (or dance) down the middle

Lead (or dance) down the middle is usually danced by individual couples but can sometimes involve three or four dancers. Dancers may lead (or dance) down the middle for one, two, three, or four steps. If dancers lead down the middle, right hands are given. If dancers dance down the middle, nearer hands are given. This may be danced with one travelling step (see below) or two walking steps to each bar. Lead (or dance) up is in the opposite direction.

Figure of eight
Figure of eight is a formation danced round standing dancers and can be up and down the set or across the set. It takes eight bars of music (sixteen counts).

For a figure of eight up and down the set, dancers pass the first standing dancer by the right, dance round the next dancers by the left, the first dancer by the right again, and return to place. A figure of eight may also begin passing by the left.

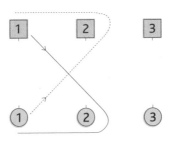

For a figure of eight across the set, dancers cross diagonally (up or down), dance round the dancer on the opposite side, cross diagonally (up or down), and return to place.

A half figure of eight takes four bars and the dancers finish in opposite places.

Rights and Lefts
A formation for two couples, which takes eight bars of music (sixteen counts).

Rights and lefts are a mini grand chain with the dancers moving along the sides of a square.

Starting position.

Bars
1 – 2	Give right hand to partner to change places.
3 – 4	Give left hand to other man or woman to change places on opposite sides.

5 – 6	Giving right hand to partner, cross back.
7 – 8	Give left hand to other man or woman to change places on own sides: all now in original places.

Hands Across

A formation for two couples which takes eight bars of music: it is often called a wheel or a star.

Bars

1 – 4	Joining right hands with the diagonally opposite dancer and keeping the two pairs of hands together, all dance round for four steps (eight counts), release hands, and turn inwards to face the opposite direction.
5 – 8	Joining left hands with the diagonally opposite dancer and keeping the two pairs of hands together, all dance round to original place.

Set and Hands Across Halfway

A formation for two couples, which takes eight bars of music (sixteen counts).

Bars

1 – 2	Join nearer hands on the side and set.
3 – 4	Giving right hands into a wheel (star), dance halfway round to finish on opposite side.
5 – 6	Join nearer hands on the opposite side and set.
7 – 8	Giving left hands into a wheel (star), dance halfway round to finish back to original position.

Poussette

A poussette is a form of progression. It takes eight bars of music. It is danced by two couples, facing their partner with both hands joined, standing side by side in the middle of the set. They end by changing positions and use a setting step throughout.

Bars

1 – 2   Top couple dance towards the men's side and make a quarter turn clockwise, while the bottom couple dance towards the ladies' side and make a quarter turn clockwise.

3 – 4   Both couples move up or down the side lines to change positions (top couple moving down on men's side and second couple moving up on the ladies' side) and make a quarter turn clockwise

5 – 6   Both couples dance into the centre of the set (now side by side, having changed places) and make a half turn back to their own side of the dance (still in centre of set).

7 – 8   All dance backwards, away from partner to their own side.

Promenade

A promenade is danced by two or three couples. It takes eight bars of music.

Couples stand beside partner in the middle of the set facing the top, men with their partner on their right, and join both hands, left in left, right in right, and the right above left.

Bars

1 – 2	Dance one step forward and slightly to the right, wheel round to the left to face the men's side.
3 – 4	Moving to the left, dance across the top of the set, to face down on the men's side and start dancing down the men's side.
5 – 6	Dance into the centre of the set facing up.
7 – 8	Dance up the centre and back to original place.

Reel of three

A reel of three is danced by three dancers. It can be danced across the set, on the side of the set or on a diagonal. It can take six or eight bars of music. The pattern, if drawn on the floor, forms a figure of eight (see fig).

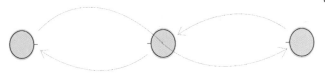

Reel of four

A reel of four is danced by four dancers. It can be danced across the set, on the side of the set, or on a diagonal. It takes eight bars of music.

Dancers will be in a line of four with the two in the middle back to back (see fig).

Turn

A turn involves two dancers and can be danced with right, left, or both hands. Dancers face each other and, giving hands, move round each other back to place.

This can also be a swing turn, pivot, or birl; dancers must ensure that they finish at the correct time and in the correct position.

Easy Ceilidh Dances

In this section the dances have all been selected on the basis that they are the type of dance that might be danced at a typical ceilidh dance. They include the well-known Scottish dances such as the Gay Gordons and the Eightsome Reel, as well as some less well-known dances. They cover a wide range of dance types including round-the-room couple dances, simple longwise set dances, and dances in square sets. They are nearly all dances that can be easily and quickly learnt.

Bluebell Polka

Couple side by side, both facing the line of dance in open hold, dance with nearer hands joined, men with their partners on their right.

Music: Polka, preferably own tune

Four counts per bar.

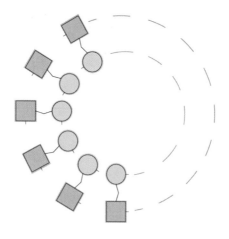

Bars

1   Starting with outside foot, point side, point in, point front, point in (with hops).

2   Woman crosses in from of partner (right, left, right, hop) to finish on his left-hand side, both still facing the line of dance.

3 – 4   Repeat bars 1 – 2, but finish with woman in front of man, facing them. Man facing line of dance.

5 – 6   Taking ballroom hold, or with both hands joined, dance in the direction of line of dance: man forward left, right, left, hop, right, left, right, hop, and woman right, left, right, hop, left, right, left, hop.

7 – 8   In ballroom hold, turn with four step hops along the line of dance, opening out ready to start again.

        Repeat.

Source: Dance originally devised by Johnny Coombs.

Boston Two Step

Couple side by side both facing the line of dance in open hold, with nearer hands joined, men with their partners on their right.

Music: 6/8 marches

Two counts per bar.

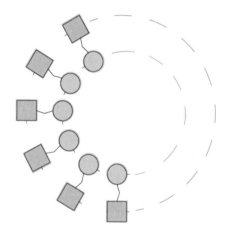

Bars

1 – 4   Starting with outside foot, set away from partner, set towards partner, starting with outside foot, walk forward for three steps and turn towards partner to face against the line of dance.

5 – 8   Repeat bars 1 – 4 back to original place and finish facing partner with both hands joined.

9 – 10   Set to partners (or alternative use jump and kick step, right and left).

11 – 12 Chasse along the line of dance to the man's left.

13 – 16 Taking ballroom hold, dance a waltz turn, opening out to finish ready to begin again.

Repeat.

The Boston Two Step has a number of regional variations.

Source: Dance originally devised by Tom Walton.

Bridge of Athlone

Sets of five couples in longwise formation. Men stand with left shoulder to top of room, women on opposite side of the set facing partner. After one turn through the dance the top couple finish at the bottom of the set. A new top couple begins.

Music: 5 x 48 bar jig

2 counts per bar.

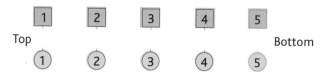

Bars

1 – 4   All join hands on the sidelines, advance and retire.

5 – 8   Men join hands on the side and raise arms to make arches and all cross over to the opposite side, women dancing under arches.

9 – 16   Repeat bars 1 – 8, women making the arches.

17 – 24   First couple join both hands and dance eight slip steps (gallop) down the middle and eight up to place.

25 – 32   First couple followed by second, third,
          fourth, and fifth couples cast off to the
          bottom of the set and first couple make
          an arch.
          Second, third, fourth, and fifth couples
          meet partners, join nearer hands, and
          dance up under the arch to new places,
          staying in the middle. Join both hands
          with partners and make an arch.
          First couple are at the bottom of the set.

33 – 36   First woman dances up under the arches
          while her partner dances up outside on
          the men's side.

37 – 40   First man dances down under the
          arches while first woman dances down
          outside on the women's side.
          First couple stay at the bottom of the set.

41 – 48   All join hands with partners and
          turn/swing, to finish on the sidelines
          ready to start again.

          Repeat with new top couple.

Source: Traditional.

The Britannia Two Step

Threes (either one man with two women
or one woman with two men) all
facing the line of dance with
hands joined.

Music: 6/8 marches

Two counts per bar.

Bars

1 – 4   With nearer hands joined, touch the left
          heel, then the left toe, to the floor, hopping
          on the right foot with each touch, all slip
          step to the left for two steps. Repeat with
          opposite foot, moving to the right.

5 – 8   Walk forward for three steps and swing
          right leg and then backwards for three steps
          and stop.

9 – 12   All set and outside partners turn towards
          centre partner and under their raised arms

13 – 16   All walk forward for three steps and swing,
           and then backwards for three steps and
           swing.
           Repeat.

Source: Original source unknown, published in
Collins Pocket Reference guide to Scottish Country
Dancing (1996).

Canadian Barn Dance

Couple side by side both facing the line of dance in open hold dance with nearer hands joined, men with their partners on their right.

Music: 6/8 or 2/4 marches

When this is danced to 2/4 pipe marches it is frequently known as the Highland Barn dance.

Two counts per bar.

Description here is for 6/8 music. When danced to 2/4 marches, the whole dance takes eight bars with four counts per bar.

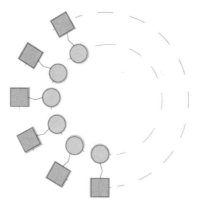

Bars

1 – 4   Starting with outside foot, walk forward for three steps and hop, walk backwards for three steps and hop.

5 – 8   Step, close, step, away from partner and clap, step, close, step, towards partner and clap (men towards the centre, women outwards). Return to partner in waltz hold.

9 – 12   Chasse sideways to the man's left for two steps and back.

13 – 16 Taking ballroom hold, polka (step hop on alternate feet) round the room along the line of dance.

Repeat.

Source: Dance originally devised by B Durrands and published in Collins Pocket Reference guide to Scottish Country Dancing (1996).

Circassian Circle

Couples form a large circle, all facing the centre, men with their partners on their left. The dance is progressive, with the man dancing with a new partner for each turn.

Music: 32 bar reels

Two counts per bar.

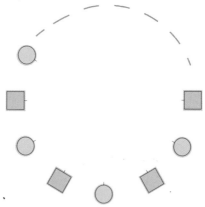

Bars

1 – 4   All join hands in the circle and advance four walking steps and retire four walking steps.

5 – 8   Repeat bars 1 – 4.

9 – 12	Release hands, women advance four walking steps, clap, and retire four walking steps.
13 – 16	Men advance four walking steps, clap, pulling back by the left, turn to face partner, i.e. dancer on the man's left.
17 – 20	All set twice to new partner (or dance back to back).
21 – 24	All, giving right hand to new partner, turn to finish in promenade hold (woman on man's right) facing the line of dance (this is frequently done with the dancers swinging in ballroom hold).
25 – 32	All promenade along line of dance for sixteen walking steps. All finish back in large circle with the man's partner on his right.

Note: All the women have now moved on one place with the woman on the man's left being his 'new' partner for the next turn through the dance.

Repeat.

Source: Traditional and published by RSCDS in Dance Trad.

The Circle Waltz

Couples form a large circle, all facing the centre, men with their partners on their right. The dance is progressive with the man dancing with a new partner for each turn.

Music: 32-bar waltz

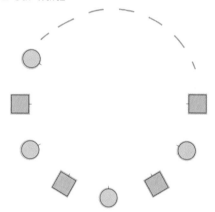

Bars

1 – 2   All take hands in large circle and take one step towards centre and out again.

3 – 4   Man dancing on the spot, releases his partner's hand, and assists the woman on

his left to dance across in front of him, passing face to face, to finish on his right: all finish facing in.

5 – 16   Repeat bars 1 – 4 three more times.

17 – 18   Man faces the woman on the right, takes both hands, steps towards centre man left, woman right, and swings free foot in front. Repeat on the other foot back to places.

19 – 20   Dancing towards centre, turn away from partner: man anticlockwise, woman clockwise (turn single).

21 – 24   Repeat bars 17 – 20 away from centre.

25 – 28   Taking ballroom hold chasse to centre and away from centre.

29 – 32   In ballroom hold, dance a waltz turn, opening out to re-form circle.

Repeat.

Source: Originally devised by Alex Moore and published in Collins Pocket Reference guide to Scottish Country Dancing (1996).

Cumberland Reel

Sets of four couples in longwise formation, men stand with left shoulder to top of room, women on opposite side of the set, facing partner. After one turn through the dance the top couple finish at the bottom of the set. A new top couple begins.

Music: 4 x 32 bar jig

Two counts per bar.

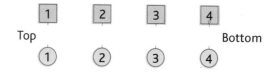

Bars

1 – 8   First and second couples dance right hands across and left hands back.

9 – 16   First couple lead down the middle and back.

17 – 28   First couple, followed by second, third, and fourth couples, cast off on own sides to the bottom of the set, meet, and lead back up to original places.

29 – 32   Second, third, and fourth couples make an arch and the first couple dance under the arches to the bottom of the set.

Repeat with new top couple.

Source: Collected locally and RSCDS Book 1.

The Cumberland Square Eight

Four couples in a square set, men with their partners on their right.

Music: 2 x 64 bar reel

Two counts per bar.

In this dance the couples in first and third places are frequently referred to as head couples and the couples in second and fourth places as side couples.

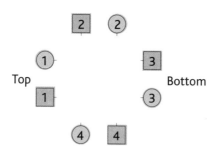

Bars

1 – 8   First and third couples (head couples), taking both hands with partner, dance eight slip steps (gallop) across the set,

men passing back to back, then eight slip steps back to place, women passing back to back.

9 – 16   Second and fourth couples (side couples) repeat bars 1 – 8.

17 – 24 First and 3rd couples dance right hands across (eight walking steps), and dance left hands across (eight walking steps) back to place.

25 – 32 Second and fourth couples repeat bars 17 – 24.

33 – 40 First and third couples meeting in the middle of the set, dance the basket – men grasp wrists firmly behind women's waists. At the same time, women take hands and raise them over the men's heads to finish with hands joined behind the men's backs.

In this formation, circle round to the left using a pivot step. Finish in original places.

41 – 48 Second and fourth couples repeat bars 33 – 40.

49 – 56 All join hands and circle round to the left and back.

57 – 64   All join hands with partner, face anticlockwise with men on the inside, and promenade round the set (sixteen steps). Finish in original places.

Repeat with side couples leading.

Source: Traditional and published by RSCDS in Dance Trad.

The Dashing White Sergeant

Three facing three round the room (man with two women or a woman with two men).

Music: 32 bar reel – 'The Dashing White Sergeant'

Two counts per bar.

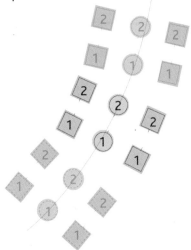

Bars

1 – 8   All circle six hands round to the left and back to the right. Finish in original lines of three.

9 – 12	The middle dancer in each group of three faces the right-hand partner, set to each other and, giving right hands, turns or swings once round. The left-hand partner stands still.
13 – 16	Facing left-hand partner, repeat bars 9 – 12.
17 – 24	Dance reels of three, the centre dancer passes the right-hand partner's left shoulder to begin. (A common variation is for the centre dancer to turn or swing each of their partners in turn, beginning right hand with the right-hand partner, then left hand to the left-hand partner.)
25 – 28	Joining hands, in lines of three, advance and retire.
29 – 32	Both lines dance forward, one line raising their hands in an arch and the other line dancing underneath, and dance on to meet the next line of three coming in the other direction.
	Repeat with the next three dancers.

Source: Attributed to David Anderson, Dundee (c 1897) and RSCDS Book 3.

Dunedin Festival Dance

Three couples in a circle round the room, men with their partners on their right

Music: 32 bar reel

Two counts per bar.

Bars

1 – 8   All three couples dance six hands round to the left and back to the right.

9 – 12   All three couples face their partners and dance back to back (do-si-do), passing by the right to begin.

13 – 16   All, giving right hands, turn partner once round.

17 – 20   All, joining right hand with the person opposite (this dancer will be your new partner) dance right hands across once round.

| 21 – 24 | The man whose hand is underneath takes the woman opposite (his new partner) under the hands of the others and they take promenade hold. The next man does the same, and the third man takes his new partner towards him in promenade hold. |
| 25 – 32 | Promenade in any direction round the room and find another two couples to form a new circle. |

Repeat with new partner.

Note this dance can be danced with more than three couples in the set.

Source: Adapted from the dance 'Borrowdale Exchange' for Dunedin Dancers in 1991 and published in Collins Pocket Reference guide to Scottish Country Dancing (1996).

The Eightsome Reel

Four couples in a square set, men with their partners on their right. Couple with their backs to the music are couple number one, couple on their left number two, couple opposite number three, and couple on the right number four.

Music: Reels, played forty bars for the chorus, then plus 8 x 48 and for the figure and forty bars for the final chorus.

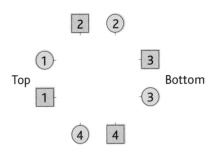

Bars: **Chorus:**

1 – 8   All circle eight hands round to the left and back to the right.

9 – 12   All women join right hands in the middle, and holding partners round waist, all dance right hands across.

81

13 – 16	Still retaining arms round partners' waists, swing the men into centre and dance left across back to places.
17 – 20	All face partner and set twice.
21 – 24	All, giving right hand (or swing hold) turn or swing partners, finish in original places facing partner.
25 – 40	Giving right hands to partner to start, dance a grand chain round the set, men dancing anticlockwise and women dancing clockwise. Give left hand to the next dancer, and continue to original places.

Figure – repeat eight times

1 – 8	First woman moves into the centre of the set and dances setting steps while the others circle round to the left and back.
9 – 16	First woman sets to partner, turns him, sets to opposite man, and turns him.
17 – 24	First woman, first man, and third man dance a reel of three, passing partner right shoulder to begin. (Variation – first woman turns or swings first man and third man in turn, beginning right hand

with their partner, then left hand to the opposite man)

25 – 32   Repeat bars 1 – 8.

33 – 48   Repeat bars 9 – 24 with fourth man and second man.

This 48-bar figure is repeated with the second woman, third woman, fourth woman, first man, second man, third man, fourth man in the centre.

Chorus: Repeat bars 1 – 40 of the Chorus.

Source: It is said that this dance was devised by the Earl of Dunmore and some of his friends in the 1870s from their recollection of older round reels. The chorus for the dance, which is danced both at the start and end is made up of typical quadrille formations, while the central portion of the dance is based on Scottish reel figures, with a series of setting and reels of three. It became popular throughout the whole of Scotland and remains one of the archetypal Scottish dances to this day.

Eva Three Step

Couple side by side, both facing the line of dance in open hold dance with nearer hands joined, men with their partners on their right.

Music: 6/8 marches

Two counts per bar.

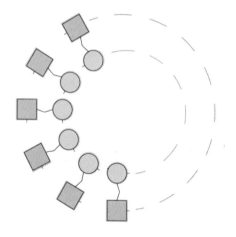

Bars

1 – 2   Couple take three steps forward and close feet together or kick with free leg.

3 – 4	Walk three steps sideways and close feet together, the man moving to his right, behind his partner, and woman moving to her left, in front of partner. They are now in each other's places.
5 – 6	Repeat bars 3 – 4 in opposite direction back to places with man now passing in front of woman.
7 – 8	Couple take three steps backward and close.
9 – 12	Couple, moving along line of dance turn away from each other (back to back) and then forward again to face partners.
13 – 16	Taking ballroom hold, the couples dance a waltz turn to finish ready to begin again.

Repeat.

Note: there are quite a few variations to this dance, particularly in bars 9 – 12.

Source: Originally devised by Sydney W Painter for his daughter Eve and published in Collins Pocket Reference guide to Scottish Country Dancing (1996).

The Flying Scotsman

Sets of four couples in longwise formation, men stand with left shoulder to top of room, women on opposite side of the set facing partner. After one turn through the dance the top couple finish at the bottom of the set. A new top couple begins.

Music: 4 x 32 bar jig

Two counts per bar.

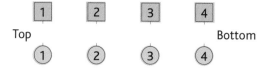

There are several versions of this, a common one is:

Bars

1 – 8 First woman, followed by second and third women, dances across the top of the set, behind first man, in front of second man, behind third man, and across the set and back to place.

9 – 16	First three men repeat bars 1 – 8 round the women.
17 – 24	First couple join both hands and dance (gallop) down the room for eight slip steps, then back up again to the bottom of the set (fourth place).
25 – 32	All four couples join hands on the sides and slip step down the room and back up again (frequently making train noises).

Finish in the order 2, 3, 4, 1.

Repeat with new top couple.

Source: Devised by Hugh A Thurston and published by the RSCDS in Jigs and Reels.

The Gay Gordons

Couple facing the line of dance in allemande hold
i.e. men with their partner on their right and with
both hands joined, left in left, right in right, and the
right above left. The man raises his partner's right
hand over her head to hold it just above, but not
resting on, her right shoulder. The left hands and
arms are held away from the body.

Music: 4/4 or 6/8 marches

Two counts per bar.

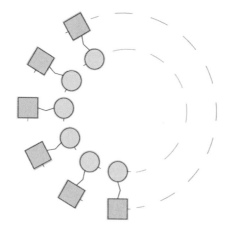

Bars

1 – 2 In allemande hold, walk forward for four steps along the line of dance, starting on the right foot.

3 – 4 Still moving in the same direction and retaining hands, each dancer turns on the spot (so left hands are joined behind woman's left shoulder and right hands joined in front) and take four steps walking backwards in the same direction, along the line of dance.

5 – 8 Repeat bars 1 – 4 in the opposite direction, against the line of dance.

9 – 12 Releasing left hands, raise right hands above woman's head, the man walks forward as the woman turns under his arm. (A common variation is for both dancers to set away from partner and back.)

13 – 16 Taking ballroom hold, the couple dance a waltz turn to finish, ready to begin again.

Repeat.

Source: Traditional and published in Collins Pocket Reference guide to Scottish Country Dancing (1996).

Gay Gordons Two Step

Couple side by side, both facing the line of dance in open hold dance with nearer hands joined, men with their partners on their right.

Music: 6/8 or 4/4 marches

Two counts per bar.

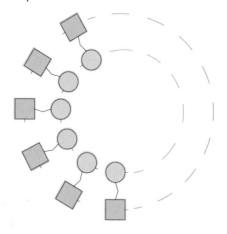

Bars

1 – 2   Beginning with the outside foot (man's left, woman's right) the dancers walk forward for four steps.

3 – 4	The man raises his right arm whilst the woman turns underneath (anti-clockwise) and both finish facing against the line of dance.
5 – 6	Repeat bars 1 – 2 in opposite direction: against line of dance and starting with the outside foot (man's right, woman's left).
7 – 8	The man raises his right arm while the woman turns underneath (anticlockwise) and both finish facing along the line of dance.
9 – 10	Releasing hands, the dancers each make one full turn away from their partners (women clockwise, men anticlockwise).
11 – 12	Face each other and set using two pas de basque steps.
13 – 16	Couples dance back to back (do-si-do) with their partners.

Repeat.

Note: There are several variations for bars 13 – 16 of this dance.

Source: Traditional.

Good-Hearted Glasgow

Sets of four couples in longwise formation, men stand with left shoulder to top of room, women on opposite side of the set facing partner. After one turn through the dance, the top couple finish in second place and repeat the dance from this position, dancing with the two couples below them, and finish at the bottom of the set. A new top couple begins.

Music: 8 x 32 bar jig

Two counts per bar.

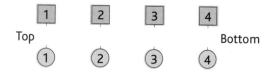

Bars

1 – 4   First couple, giving right hands, turn once round and cast off one place on their own sides. Second couple step up.

5 – 8   First couple, giving left hands, turn one and a quarter times to finish in the middle of the set, facing opposite sides.

9 – 12   First woman with second couple and first man with third couple, dance right hands

across once round. On bar 12, first couple pass by the right in the middle of the set.

13 – 16   First man with second couple and first woman with third couple, dance left hands across once round. First couple finish in second place on own sides.

17 – 24   First couple lead down the middle and back to second place.

25 – 32   Second, first, and third couples dance six hands round to the left and back to the right.

Repeat with first couple starting in second position, dancing with third and fourth couples. First couple finish at the bottom.

Repeat with a new top couple.

Source: Devised by Peter Knapman and published in Collins Pocket Reference guide to Scottish Country Dancing (1996). This dance was the winning entry in a competition for a dance that would encourage people to find enjoyable ways of taking exercise as part of the Glasgow 'Good Hearted Glasgow' health education programme.

Gypsy Tap

Couple facing each other in ballroom hold, men with their backs to the centre of the room and left shoulder facing line of dance.

Music: 4/4 marches

Two counts per bar.

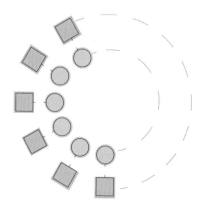

Bars

1 – 2   Take two side steps along the line of dance.

3 – 4   Still in ballroom hold, open out slightly to face the line of dance, take three smaller steps along the line of dance, starting with the outside foot (men: left, right through,

left and close, and women: right, left through, right and close).

The effect of the steps in bars 1 – 4 is slow, slow, quick, quick, quick.

5 – 8   Repeat bars 1 – 4 still in of line of dance.

9 – 16   Repeat bars 1 – 8 in opposite direction: against the line of dance.

17 – 20 With nearer hands joined and facing the line of dance, swing inside arms forward and back and, releasing hands, make a full turn away from partner, finish with nearer hands joined facing line of dance (men anticlockwise and women clockwise).

21 – 24 Repeat bars 17 – 20 still facing line of dance.

25 – 28 Chasse along line of dance then chasse against line of dance.

29 – 32 Taking ballroom hold, the couple dance a waltz turn to finish ready to begin again.

Repeat.

Source: Devised by Professor Bollett, in the 1920s in Sydney Australia.

Hesitation Waltz

Couple facing each other in ballroom hold, men with their backs to the centre of the room and left shoulder facing line of dance.

Music: Waltz

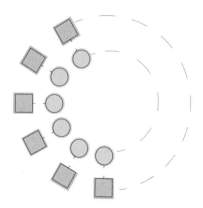

Bars

1 – 2   Chasse to man's left, moving along the line of dance.

3 – 4   Repeat bars 1 – 2 against line of dance.

5 – 8   Move along the line of dance.

Man steps left, right through, left, right close, while woman steps right, left through, right, left close.

Finish alongside partner with man facing line of dance and woman facing against line of dance.

9 – 12   Dance against line of dance for three steps with a slight 'dip' on four (men: right, left, right, then 'dip' and women: left, right, left, then 'dip').

13 – 16   Taking ballroom hold, the couples dance a waltz turn to finish ready to begin again.

Repeat.

Source: Devised by John Evans and published in Collins Pocket Reference guide to Scottish Country Dancing (1996).

Highland Schottische

Couple facing each other in ballroom hold, men with their backs to the centre of the room and left shoulder facing line of dance. Note: this dance is frequently danced in an open hold, both facing the line of dance and arms round partner's waist, men with partner on their right.

Music: Schottische

Four counts per bar.

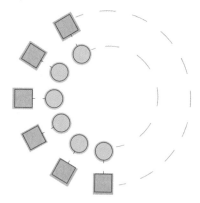

Bars

1   Men with left foot, women with right, point foot in direction of line of dance, bring foot towards instep of supporting foot, repeat.

	Hop on supporting foot on each of these four counts.
2	Take two sidesteps along line of dance, man starting with left foot, woman with right, hopping on front foot on count four (step, close, step, hop).
3 – 4	Repeat bars 1 – 2 in opposite direction against the line of dance.
5	Take two sidesteps along line of dance, man starting with left foot, woman with right, hopping on front foot on count four (step, close, step, hop).
6	Repeat bar 5 in opposite direction against the line of dance.
7 – 8	In ballroom hold, polka, rotating clockwise and following line of dance anticlockwise around the room (step, hop, step, hop, step, hop, step).
	Repeat.

Source: The Highland Schottische was introduced in the 1850s, was initially known as the 'Balmoral Schottische', and was published in Collins Pocket Reference guide to Scottish Country Dancing (1996).

A Highland Welcome

Couple facing couple round the room, men with their partners on their right.

Music: 32 bar reel

Two counts per bar.

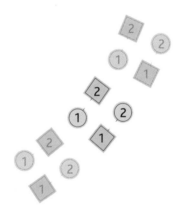

Bars

1 – 8   All circle to the left for eight slip steps and back to the right for eight slip steps.

9 – 16   All dance right hands across for four bars (eight counts) and then dance left hands across back to places.

17 – 20   All, giving left hand to dancer opposite, turn or swing once round and finish facing partner.

21 – 24   All, giving right hand to partner, turn or swing once round and finish facing opposite couple.

25 – 28   Joining nearer hand with partner, walk forward for four steps and retire four steps.

29 – 32   Couples facing clockwise make an arch. All walk forward for eight steps and the couples facing anticlockwise pass under the arch made by the other couples, to meet a new couple.

Repeat with new couple.

Source: Devised by Bill Forbes and published in Collins Pocket Reference guide to Scottish Country Dancing (1996).

Lomond Waltz

Couple facing each other in ballroom hold, men with their backs to the centre of the room and left shoulder facing line of dance.

Music: Waltz – frequently danced to 'Loch Lomond' played in waltz time.

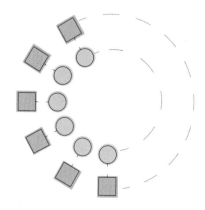

Bars

1 – 2   Take two side steps (left, close, right) along the line of dance (to the man's left).

3 – 4   Take two steps towards centre, man moving backwards and starting with right foot, woman starting with left foot.

5 – 6	Take two steps against the line of dance (to man's right).
7 – 8	Take two steps out from the centre, man moving forward and starting with left foot, woman starting with right foot.
9 – 10	Joining nearer hands (man's right, woman's left), make a half turn (man anticlockwise and woman clockwise) to finish back to back.
11 – 12	Continue the turn to finish facing partner.
13 – 16	With both hands joined, balance forward and back and change places, the woman turning under the man's raised left hand.
17 – 20	Repeat bars 13 – 16 back to original sides.
21 – 24	With both hands joined and moving along line of dance, side step as follows:

Man – side step left, cross right foot through, point left foot along the line of dance, and close.

Woman uses opposite foot – side step right, cross left foot through, point right foot along the line of dance, and close.

25 – 28   Bars 21 – 24 are repeated against the line
          of dance.
29 – 32   Taking ballroom hold, the couples dance a
          waltz turn to finish ready to begin again.
          Repeat.

Source: Originally devised by Botham and published
in Collins Pocket Reference guide to Scottish Country
Dancing (1996).

The Marmalade Sandwich

Sets of four couples in longwise formation, men stand with left shoulder to top of room, women on opposite side of the set facing partner. After one turn through the dance the top couple finish at the bottom of the set. A new top couple begins.

Music: 4 x 48 bar reel

Two counts per bar.

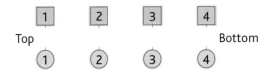

Bars

1 – 8   All four women, led by first woman, dance across the top of the set, down behind the men's line, across the bottom of the set and up the sideline to original places.

9 – 16   All four men, led by first man, dance across the top of the set, down behind the women's line, across the bottom of the set, and up the sideline to original places.

17 – 20	All dance back to back (do-si-do) with partner.
21 – 24	All, giving right hand to partner, turn once round.
25 – 32	First couple join both hands and dance eight slip steps down the middle and eight back to place.
33 – 36	First couple cast off one place and, giving right hand to partner, turn once round. At the same time, the other three couples, without joining hands, advance and clap partners' hands and retire to place: second couple retire diagonally to first place.
37 – 40	First couple, now in second place, cast off one place and, giving right hand to partner, turn once round. Second, third, and fourth couples repeat bars 33 – 36. Third couple retire diagonally to second place.
41 – 44	First couple, now in third place, cast off one place and, giving right hand to partner, turn once round.

Second, third, and fourth couples repeat bars 33 – 36.

Fourth couple retire diagonally to third place. First couple are now in fourth place.

45 – 48 All, giving right hands, turn or swing partners.

Repeat with new top couple.

Source: Devised by Ian Brockbank and published by RSCDS in Dance Trad.

The Military Two Step

Couple side by side, both facing the line of dance in open hold, with nearer hands joined, men with their partners on their right.

Music: 6/8 marches or two step

Two counts per bar.

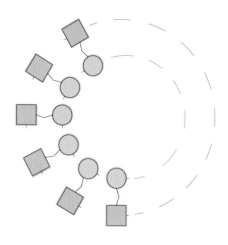

Bars

1 – 4   With outside foot, tap heel forward, then toe, and repeat, walk forward for three steps, and turn towards partner to face against the line of dance.

5 – 8   Repeat bars 1 – 4 back to starting place and finish facing partner with both hands joined.

9 – 10   Jump and kick right foot, jump and kick left foot (or set).

11 – 12   Man turns his partner under his raised right arm.

13 – 16   Taking ballroom hold, the couples dance a waltz turn to finish ready to begin again.

Repeat.

Source: Originally devised by James Finnigan and published in Collins Pocket Reference guide to Scottish Country Dancing (1996).

The Mississippi Dip

Couple dance, men with back to the centre of the room, left shoulder to line of dance. Start in ballroom hold, man with left foot and woman with right foot. Steps are given for the man, the woman on opposite foot.

Music: 4/4 marches

Two counts per bar.

Tune: Any hoedown tune.

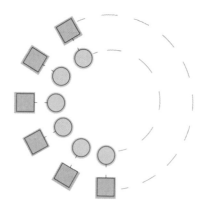

Bars

1 – 2   Three steps towards the centre of the room (left, right, left, close).

3 – 4   Balance (sway) left and right (along the line of dance and against the line of dance – 2 slow steps).

5 – 6   Three steps away from the centre (left, right, left close).

7 – 8   Balance (sway) left and right (along the line of dance and against the line of dance – 2 slow steps).

9 – 10   Three steps along the line of dance (left, right, left, close). The woman turns to face against the line of dance.

11 – 12   Three steps against the line of dance, woman forward and man backwards.

13 – 16   Rotary waltz turn, finish in open hold, both facing line of dance.

17 – 20   Step left, step right with a slight dip, step left, right together, back left together, along the line of dance.

21 – 24   Repeat bars 17 – 20, again along the line of dance.

25 – 26	Chasse along the line of dance (man's left).
27 – 28	Chasses against the line of dance (man's right).
29 – 32	Rotary waltz turn to finish with man's back to centre.
	Repeat.

Source: Originally devised by Charles Wood and published in Collins Pocket Reference guide to Scottish Country Dancing (1996).

OXO Reel

Sets of six couples in longwise formation, men stand with left shoulder to top of room, women on opposite side of the set facing partner. Each couple dances the dance once through to finish at the bottom of the set. A new top couple begin.

Music: 6 x 32 bar reel

Two counts per bar.

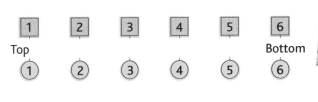

Bars

1 – 4   All join hands on the sides, advance, and retire.

5 – 8   First couple join both hands and dance eight slip steps to the bottom of the set and finish on own side.

9 – 12   All join hands on the sides, advance, and retire.

13 – 16   Second couple, who are now at the top, dance with eight slip steps to the bottom of the set and finish on own side.

17 – 24   The top two couples and the bottom two couples, dance four hands round to the left and back to the right, while the middle two couples dance right hands across and left hands back.

25 – 28   Second couple, at the bottom of the set, join both hands and dance with eight slip steps up to the top.

29 – 32   All turn or swing partner, moving up slightly to keep the set in the original place, and finish on the sidelines ready to start again.

Repeat with new top couple.

Source: John Tether and published by the RSCDS in Dance Trad.

The Packhorse Rant

Couple facing couple round the room, men with their partners on their right.

Music: 32 bar reel

Two counts per bar.

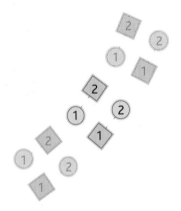

Bars

1 – 8   All dance right hands across once round, for eight walking steps, and dance a left hands across back to place.

9 – 12   Women dance back to back (do-si-do), passing by the right to begin.

13 – 16   Men dance back to back (do-si-do), passing by the right to begin.

17 – 20   Join both hands with partner and, with men passing back to back, slip step past the other couple, and on round the room.

21 – 24   Return to place, women passing back to back, and finish in original places facing the same couple.

25 – 28   Joining nearer hand with partner, walk forward for four steps and retire four steps.

29 – 32   Couples facing clockwise make an arch. All walk forward for eight steps and the couples facing anticlockwise pass under the arch made by the other couples, to meet a new couple.

Repeat with new couple.

Source: Ian Brockbank and published by the RSCDS in Dance Trad.

Postie's Jig

Sets of four couples in longwise formation, men
stand with left shoulder to top of room, women on
opposite side of the set facing partner. Both the
first and fourth couples are the dancing couples,
finishing with the first couple in third place and the
fourth couple in second place.

Music: 4 x 32 bar jig

Two counts per bar.

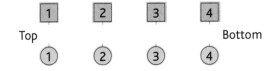

Top   Bottom

Bars

1 – 2   First and fourth couples set.

2 – 4   First couple cast off one place while
         fourth couple cast up one place. Second
         couple step up to top place while third
         couple step down to fourth place.

5 – 8   First couple dance a half figure eight round
         second couple while fourth couple dance a
         half figure eight round third couple.

9 – 12   First man with fourth man and first woman
           with fourth woman, take nearer hands and
           cross to the opposite side of the set: the
           men making an arch for the women to
           dance under. Give free hand to corner
           person and turn, i.e. first man to second
           man and first woman to second woman, etc.
           Corners finish in places, while first couple
           meet and join nearer hands to face down
           and fourth couple meet and join nearer
           hands to face up.

13 – 16   First couple and fourth couple, with nearer
           hands joined, change places up and down,
           the fourth couple making an arch for the
           first couple to dance under. Give free hand
           to corner person and turn, i.e. first man to
           third man and first woman to third woman,
           etc. Corners finish in places, while first and
           fourth men meet and join nearer hands on
           own side and first and fourth women meet
           and join hands on own side.

17 – 24   Repeat the pattern of crossing and
           turning as in bars 9 – 12 and 13 – 16.
           When changing places across the set,

the men always make the arches and, when changing up and down the set, the couple dancing up always make the arch. Finish in the order 2, 1, 4, 3, with the first and fourth couples on opposite sides.

25 – 28   First and fourth couples dance half rights and lefts.

29 – 32   First and fourth couples turn by the right hand once round to finish in the order 2, 4, 1, 3.

Repeat with new top couple.

Source: Devised by Roy Clowes and published in Collins Pocket Reference guide to Scottish Country Dancing (1996).

Pride of Erin Waltz

Couple side by side, both facing the line of dance in open hold, with nearer hands joined, men with partner on their right.

Music: Waltz

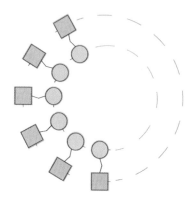

Bars

1 – 4   Facing the line of dance with nearer hands joined, swing the inner leg forward and back, then walk forward for three steps. Finish by turning towards partner to face in opposite direction, against the line of dance.

5 – 8   Repeat bars 1 – 4 against the line of dance.

9 – 10   Join hands, facing partner, man moves to right by crossing left foot over right,

then points right foot to side, while woman moves to her left by crossing right foot over left and pointing left foot to side.

11 – 12 Repeat bars 9 – 10 in opposite direction.

13 – 16 Turn away from partner (man pulling left shoulder back and woman pulling right shoulder back by right). Complete the turn to finish facing partner.

17 – 20 With both hands joined, balance forward and back and change places, the man turning the woman under his raised right hand.

21 – 24 Repeat bars 17 – 20 back to places.

25 – 28 Taking ballroom hold or joining both hands with partner, chasse along the line of dance and then chasse against the line of dance.

29 – 32 Taking ballroom hold, the couples dance a waltz turn to finish ready to begin again.

Repeat.

Source: Originally devised by Charles Wood and published in Collins Pocket Reference guide to Scottish Country Dancing (1996).

The Riverside

One long set arranged in a series of two couples sets. In each set the first couple stand with their left shoulder to the top of the set, the second couple face the first couple on the opposite side of the set, men with their partners on their right. Each set is joined to the next to make two long lines, each line alternating men and women.

Music: 32 bar jig

Two counts per bar.

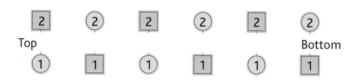

Bars

1 – 8   All join hands on the sidelines and advance for four steps and retire for four steps and repeat.

9 – 16   In the two couple sets, dance right hands across and left hands back.

17 – 20	Face partner on the sidelines and dance back to back (do-si-do) passing right shoulder to begin.
21 – 24	Face across the set and dance back to back with the opposite dancer, passing right shoulder to begin.
25 – 32	The top two couples join hands in a line of four facing down the set, men with partner on their right. Raising their arms to form arches over the two lines of dancers, they dance to the bottom of the lines.

All dancers move up two places.

Repeat with two new top couples.

Source: Devised by Karen Ingram and published by the RSCDS in Dance Trad.

Round Reel of Eight

Four couples in a square set, men with their partners on their right.

Music: 88 bar reel

Two counts
per bar.

Top

Bottom

Bars

1 – 8   All four women pull back by the right and dance clockwise round the outside of the set back to original places.

9 – 16   All four men pull back by the left and dance anticlockwise round the outside the set back to original places.

17 – 24 All four couples dance a grand chain halfway round, giving right hand to partner to begin. Set to partner.

25 – 32 Repeat bars 17 – 24 back to original places.

33 – 35 First and third couples change places. First couple, giving nearer hands, dance between third couple.

36 – 38	Third and first couples change places. Third couple, giving nearer hands, dance between first couple.
39 – 40	First and third couples, giving right hands, turn into allemande hold.
41 – 48	First and third couples dance anticlockwise round the inside of the set to original places.
49 – 64	Second and fourth couples repeat bars 33 – 48. On bars 49 – 51, second couple dance between fourth couple and on bars 52 – 54, fourth couple dance between second couple.
65 – 68	First and third couples dance half rights and lefts.
69 – 72	Second and fourth couples dance half rights and lefts.
73 – 76	First and third couples dance half rights and lefts.
77 – 80	Second and fourth couples dance half rights and lefts.
81 – 88	All four couples dance eight hands round and back.

Source: Peter Thompson 1751 and RSCDS Book 27

The Sausage Machine

Sets of four couples in longwise formation, men stand with left shoulder to top of room, women on opposite side of the set facing partner. Each couple dances the dance once through to finish at the bottom of the set. A new top couple begins.

Music: 4 x 32 bar jig

Two counts per bar.

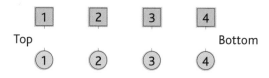

Bars

1 – 8   First couple cast to the bottom of the set, turn right hand, and cast up to original places.

9 – 16   First couple with second couple, and third couple with fourth couple, dance right hands across (eight walking steps), and left hands back.

17 – 24   All join hands in a circle and keep hands
           joined throughout:

           Fourth couple make an arch by raising
           the hand joined with partner, first couple
           followed by second and third couples,
           dance down under the arch.

           First couple, turning away from partner,
           make an arch over all the others and all
           turn away from partners, still retaining
           hands, and dance to original places.

25 – 32   First couple cast to the bottom of the set
           and turn with the right hand or swing.

           Repeat with new top couple.

Source: Published by RSCDS in Dance Trad.

Southern Rose Waltz

Couple facing each other in ballroom hold, men with their backs to the centre of the room and left shoulder facing line of dance.

Music: Waltz.

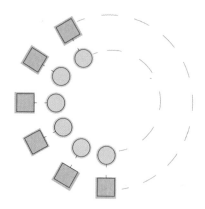

Bars

1 – 4   Side step along the line of the dance three times (step, close, step, close, step, close) and stamp lightly on the spot for two counts.

5 – 8   Woman turns away (full circle) from partner twice as the men move along the line of dance.

9 – 12   Repeat bars 1 – 4.

13 – 16   Taking ballroom hold, the couples dance
          a waltz turn to finish, men with their backs
          to the centre of the room and left shoulder
          facing line of dance, still in ballroom hold.

17 – 20   Take four steps towards the centre of the
          dance (men start with left foot moving
          back).

21 – 24   Repeat back to places.

25 – 28   Moving along the line of dance, men
          step left, right foot through, left foot point
          forward and behind with a slight dip.
          Women use opposite foot (right, left foot
          through, right foot point forward and
          behind).

29 – 32   Taking ballroom hold, the couples dance
          a waltz turn to finish ready to begin again.

          Repeat.

Source: Traditional.

St Bernard's Waltz

Couple facing each other in ballroom hold, men with their backs to the centre of the room and left shoulder facing line of dance.

Music: Waltz.

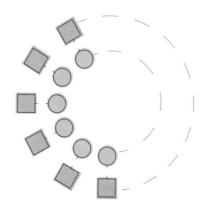

Bars

1 – 4   Side step along the line of the dance three times (step, close, step, close, step, close) and stamp lightly on the spot for two counts.

5 – 6   Take two side steps against the line of dance.

7 – 8	Take two steps towards the centre of the dance: man moving backwards starting with left foot, and woman moving forward starting with right foot.
9 – 10	Take two steps back towards the outside of the room: man starting left foot.
11 – 12	Woman turns under man's left arm while man steps to left.
13 – 16	Taking ballroom hold, the couples dance a waltz turn to finish ready to begin again.

Repeat.

Source: Traditional and published in Collins Pocket Reference guide to Scottish Country Dancing (1996).

Strip the Willow

Sets of four couples in longwise formation, men stand with left shoulder to top of room, women on opposite side of the set facing partner. Each couple dances the dance once through to finish at the bottom of the set. A new top couple begins.

Music: 6/8 or 9/8 jigs.

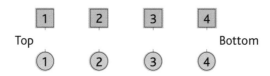

The instructions below are for 6/8 jigs, which is the more common rhythm used today. When using 9/8 jigs the phrasing of the dance described below takes forty bars of music.

Note: In this dance the turns are usually done with either a linked arm grip or an elbow grip.

Bars

1 – 8   First couple dance a pivot turn with right arm or using 'elbow grip' at the top of the set.

9 – 12	First woman turns second man left, then partner right. Repeat this pattern as follows:
13 – 16	First woman turns third man left, then partner right.
17 – 20	First woman turns fourth man left, then partner right.
21 – 24	First couple dance a pivot turn with right arm at bottom of the set.
25 – 36	First man turns fourth woman left, then partner right: this pattern is repeated with first man turning each woman, then partner, until first couple are back at the top of the set.
37 – 40	First couple dance a pivot turn with right arm at top of the set.
41 – 44	First woman turns second man left, while first man turns second woman left, then first couple turn by the right.
45 – 52	First couple continue the pattern of bars 41 – 44, turning left on the side and right to partner: first with third couple, then with fourth couple.

53 – 56   First couple dance a pivot turn with right
          arm at bottom of the set.

          Repeat with a new top couple. Note that
          the bar structure for Strip the Willow can
          be flexible and the above is a guide to the
          pattern of the dance. It is also possible to
          do the dance with more than four couples in
          the set.

Source: Traditional and RSCDS Book 1.

Orcadian Strip the Willow

Longwise sets for any number of couples, men stand with left shoulder to top of room, women on opposite side of the set facing partner.

Music: 6/8 or 9/8 jigs.

A common variant of Strip the Willow is the Orcadian Strip the Willow. This is danced as one longwise set for any number of couples. The dancing couple omit the first part of Strip the Willow and start the dance on bar 37 above, and they continue to 'strip the willow' until they reach the bottom of the set. A new top couple starts whenever the previous top couple has moved three or four places down the set. The dance is not rigidly structured but is a great way to get everyone joining in a longwise dance with enthusiasm. A loose set of instructions is given below.

No bar count is provided as the set can include any number of couples:

Part:

A   First couple dance a pivot turn with right arm or using 'elbow grip' at the top of the set for eight bars (sixteen counts).

B   Top woman turns second man left, while top man turns second woman left, then first couple turn by the right.

Top woman turns third man left, while top man turns third woman left, then first couple turn by the right.

Top woman turns fourth man left, while top man turns fourth woman left, then first couple turn by the right.

Top couple continue this pattern, right down the length of the set, until they reach the bottom, where they dance a pivot turn with right arm for a count of sixteen.

C   Once the top couple have moved down the set at least three couples, the next couple start to turn or swing at the top of the set as at 'A' above and then the 'strip the willow' as indicated in 'B' above.

D   Couples continue to follow this pattern
         with a new top couple starting every time
         the preceding couple has moved down at
         least three couples, until the original top
         couples are back at the top and the last
         couple has stripped the willow to the
         bottom of the set.

         The amount of music required for this
         dance varies depending on how many
         dancers are in the set.

Source: Traditional and published by RSCDS in
Dance Trad.

The Virginia Reel

Sets of four (or whatever the required number) couples in longwise formation, men stand with left shoulder to top of room, women on opposite side of the set facing partner. Each couple dances the dance once through to finish at the bottom of the set. A new top couple begins.

Music: 4 x 40 bar reel

Two counts per bar.

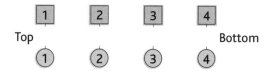

Bars

1 – 4   All advance towards partner for four walking steps and retire four walking steps.

5 – 8   Repeat bars 1 – 4.

9 – 12   All, giving right hands, turn partner once round and return to place (eight walking steps).

13 – 16   All, giving left hands, turn partner once round and return to place (eight walking steps).

17 – 20   All, giving both hands, turn partner once round and return to place (eight walking steps).

21 – 24   All dance back to back with partner (do-si-do), passing right shoulder to begin and return to place (eight walking steps).

25 – 32   First couple join both hands and dance eight slip steps down the middle and eight First couple, followed by second, third, and fourth couples, cast off to the bottom for eight walking steps. First couple join both hands to make an arch and the second, third, and fourth couples meet partner and dance under the arch for eight walking steps to re-form the set with a new top couple.

Repeat with a new top couple.

Source: Traditional and published in Collins Pocket Reference guide to Scottish Country Dancing (1996).

This dance was developed in America and is related to older traditional dances such as 'The Haymakers' (see p.140) and the English country dance 'Sir Roger de Coverley'.

Haymakers

Sets of four (or whatever the required number) couples in longwise formation, men stand with left shoulder to top of room, women on opposite side of the set facing partner. Each couple dances the dance once through to finish at the bottom of the set. A new top couple begins.

Music: 4 x 48 bar jig

Two counts per bar.

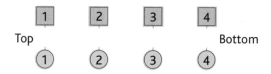

Bars

1 – 4 First woman and fourth man advance to the middle of the dance, turn with the right hand, and return to place.

5 – 8 First man and fourth woman repeat bars 1 – 4.

9 – 12	First woman and fourth man advance to the middle of the dance and turn with the left hand, and return to place.
13 – 16	First man and fourth woman repeat bars 9 – 12.
17 – 20	First woman and fourth man advance to the middle of the dance and turn with both hands, and return to place.
21 – 24	First man and fourth woman repeat bars 17 – 20.
25 – 28	First woman and fourth man advance to the middle of the dance and dance back to back passing right shoulders and return to place.
29 – 32	First man and fourth woman repeat bars 25 – 28
33 – 36	First woman and fourth man advance to the middle of the dance, curtsy or bow to each other, and retire to place.
37 – 40	First man and fourth woman repeat bars 33 – 36

41 – 48   First couple, followed by second, third, and fourth couples cast off to the bottom for eight walking steps. First couple join both hands to make an arch, and second, third, and fourth couples meet partner and dance under the arch for eight walking steps to re-form the set with a new top couple.

Repeat with new top couple.

Source: Traditional and RSCDS Book 2.

Waltz Country Dance

Couple facing couple round the room, men with their partners on their right.

Music: 40 bar waltz.

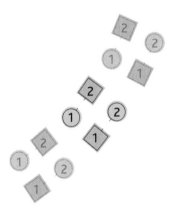

Bars

1 – 4   All advance and retire towards the opposite dancer.

All change places with opposite dancer passing right shoulder, women make a three-quarter turn by right and men a quarter turn, to finish facing partners.

5 – 8	Advance and retire towards partner and change places as in bars 1 – 4.
9 – 16	Repeat bars 1 – 8 to finish in original places.
17 – 18	All join hands in circle and balance forward and backwards.
19 – 20	Man, dancing on the spot, releases his partner's hand and assists the woman on his left to dance across in front of him, passing face to face, to finish on his right: all finish facing in.
21 – 32	Repeat bars 19 – 20 three more times: all in original positions.
33 – 40	Taking ballroom hold, the two couples dance a waltz turn to pass each other (men passing by the left) to finish facing in the original direction opposite a new couple.
	Repeat with next couple.

Source: The Ballroom (1827) and RSCDS Book 4.

More of a Challenge

The dances in this section present a bit more of a challenge. They are all country dances in longwise or square set formation. They include a few slightly more challenging formations and might take a wee bit more effort to master.

The Birks of Invermay

Sets of four couples in longwise formation. After one turn through the dance, the dancing couple finish in second place and repeat the dance from this position, dancing with the two couples below them, and finish at the bottom of the set. After two turns, the new top couple begins.

Music: 8 x 32 bar strathspey

Four counts per bar

Tune: The Birks of Invermay.

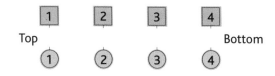

Bars

1 – 4   First man and second woman, giving both hands, turn once round.

5 – 8   First woman and second man, giving both hands, turn once round to places. On bar 8, first, second, and third couples dance

into the middle of the set to join both hands and face up.

9 – 16   First, second, and third couples dance a promenade.

17 – 24   First couple, giving right hands, cross over and cast off one place, lead up between second couple, cross over to own sides and cast off one place. Second couple step up on bars 23 – 24.

25 – 32   Second, first, and third couples dance six hands round and back.

Repeat, having passed a couple.

Source: Originally Skillern's Compleat Collection of Country Dances (1776) and RSCDS Book 16.

The Deil amang the Tailors

Sets of four couples in longwise formation. After one turn through the dance, the dancing couple finish in second place and repeat the dance from this position, dancing with the two couples below them, and finish at the bottom of the set. After two turns, the new top couple begins.

Music: 8 x 32 bar reel

Two counts per bar

Tune: The Deil amang the Tailors.

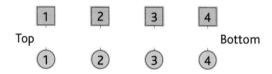

Bars

1 – 4   First and second couples, taking hands on the sides, set and dance right hands across halfway round.

5 – 8   Second and first couples, taking hands on the sides, set and dance left hands across halfway round to original places.

9 – 16   First couple lead down the middle and up to finish in the middle of the set facing up. Second couple step in behind them.

17 – 24   First and second couples dance an allemande.

25 – 32   Second, first, and third couples dance six hands round and back.

Repeat, having passed a couple.

Source: Davies Collection and RSCDS Book 14.

The Duke of Atholl's Reel

Sets of four couples in longwise formation. After one turn through the dance, the dancing couple finish in second place, repeat the dance from this position, dancing with the couple below them, and finish in third place. For the third turn of the dance, the original dancing couple repeat with the couple below them while a new top couple begin.

Music: 8 x 32 bar jig

Two counts per bar

Tune: The Athole Highlanders.

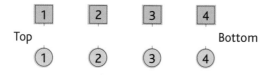

Bars

1 – 4   First and second couples, taking hands on the side, set and dance right hands across halfway round.

5 – 8	Second and first couples, taking hands on the side, set and dance left hands across back to places.
9 – 12	First man and second woman set advancing and, giving right hands, turn each other once round.
13 – 16	First woman and second man repeat bars 9 – 12.
17 – 20	First couple, giving right hands, cross over and cast off one place. Second couple step up on bars 19 – 20.
21 – 24	First couple dance a half figure of eight round second couple.
25 – 32	Second and first couples dance rights and lefts.

Repeat, having passed a couple.

Source: Originally Skillern's Compleat Collection of Country Dances (1776) and RSCDS Book 16.

Duke of Perth

Sets of four couples in longwise formation. After one turn through the dance, the dancing couple finish in second place and repeat the dance from this position, dancing with the two couples below them, and finish at the bottom of the set. After two turns, the new top couple begins.

Music: 8 x 32 bar reel

Two counts per bar

Tune: Duke of Perth's Reel.

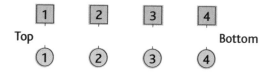

Bars

1 – 4 First couple, giving right hands, turn and cast off one place. Second couple step up on bars 3 – 4.

5 – 8 First couple, giving left hands, turn one and a quarter times to face first corners.

9 – 16	First couple turn first corners with the right hand, partner with the left hand, second corners with the right hand, and partner with the left hand, to finish facing first corners.
17 – 20	First couple set to and turn first corners to finish back to back in the middle, facing second corners.
21 – 24	First couple set to and turn second corners to finish in second place, on opposite side, facing first corners.
25 – 30	Second, first, and third couples dance reels of three on the sides. First couple pass first corners left shoulders to begin.
31 – 32	First couple, giving right hands, cross over to second place on own sides.

Repeat, having passed a couple.

This dance has been danced throughout Scotland for over 200 years and is also known as Pease Strae or Broun's Reel.

Source: The Ballroom and RSCDS Book 1.

Dunnet Head

Sets of four couples in longwise formation. After one turn through the dance, the dancing couple finish at the bottom of the set. A new top couple begins.

Music: 4 x 32 bar reel

Two counts per bar

Tune: Any good reel.

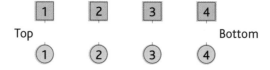

Top   Bottom

Bars

1 – 8   First woman, followed by second, third, and fourth women, dances across the top of the set, down behind the men, across the bottom of the set, and up the women's side to original place.

9 – 16   First man, followed by second, third, and fourth men, dances across the top of the set, down behind the women, across the

bottom of the set, and up the men's side to original place.

17 – 24   All dance eight hands round and back.

25 – 28   All four men and all four women, joining hands on the sides, advance and retire.

29 – 32   First couple dance down to fourth place, second, third, and fourth couples step up, on the last two bars.

Repeat with a new top couple.

Source: Peter Knight and Collins Pocket Reference guide to Scottish Country Dancing (1996).

Flowers of Edinburgh

Sets of four couples in longwise formation. After one turn through the dance, the dancing couple finish in second place and repeat the dance from this position, dancing with the two couples below them, and finish at the bottom of the set. After two turns, the new top couple begins.

Music: 8 x 32 bar reel

Two counts per bar

Tune: Flowers of Edinburgh.

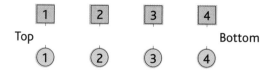

Bars

1 – 6   First woman casts off two places, crosses to the opposite side, below third couple, and dances up behind second and third men to her partner's original place. At the same time, first man follows his partner,

crossing over, and dances down behind second and third women, and up the middle to his partner's original place.

7 – 8   First couple set to each other.

9 – 14   First couple repeat bars 1 – 6, with first man casting off and first woman following. First couple finish in original places.

15 – 16   First couple set to each other.

17 – 24   First couple lead down the middle and up to finish facing each other in the middle of the set with both hands joined. Second couple step in and join both hands.

25 – 32   First and second couples dance a poussette.

Repeat, having passed a couple.

Source: The Ballroom and RSCDS Book 1.

The Glasgow Highlanders

Sets of four couples in longwise formation.

The music starts with two chords. On the second chord, first woman crosses over to the right hand side of her partner. Second man crosses to his partner's place while she moves up to first woman's place.

Music: 8 x 32 strathspey

Four counts per bar

Tune: The Glasgow Highlanders.

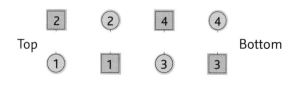

Bars

1 – 8   First and second couples dance rights and lefts.

On bar 7, second man gives his left hand to his partner and dances diagonally down into the middle, offering his right hand to first woman, who is handed over to him

158

by her partner. All face down with second man between first and second women, nearer hands joined, and first man behind second man.

9 – 12   Second man dances down the middle with first and second women followed by first man. Releasing hands, all turn to face up, first and second women turning towards second man, while first and second men turn right about.

13 – 16   First man taking nearer hands with first and second women, dances up the middle, second man following. They finish at the top in a line of four across facing partners, men back to back in the middle, and women on the sidelines.

17 – 24   First and second couples set to partners – see below.

25 – 30   First and second couples dance a reel of four across the set, passing partners by right shoulder to begin.

31 – 32   First couples progress down on the men's side of the set, while second couples progress up on the woman's side, to finish

opposite a new couple. (The men finish in their partner's original place prior to the start of that turn through the dance.)

Repeat, from new positions.

Whenever a couple reaches the top of the set, the man crosses back to his original side and stands opposite his partner for the duration of the next turn: on bars 31 and 32 the woman crosses to the man's side of the set and stands alongside her partner, ready to begin. Likewise, when couples reach the bottom of set the woman crosses back to the woman's side of the set and stands opposite her partner for the duration of the next turn: on bars 31 and 32 the woman steps up one place while her partner crosses to the woman's side of the set and stands alongside his partner ready to begin.

This dance may be danced in one continuous set, with odd numbered couples dancing down the room until they reach the bottom of the line, where they change sides, as above, and the even number couples dancing to the top of the room, where they change sides.

This dance has its own setting step, danced as follows:

Bars

1 – 2   Step forward on right foot and hop; step back on left foot and hop; step behind with right foot and step slightly to the side on left foot; step slightly forward on right foot and hop (eight counts).

3 – 4   Repeat bars 1 – 2, leading with the left foot, ie step forward on left foot and hop; step back on right foot and hop; step behind with left foot and step slightly to the side on right foot; step slightly forward on left foot and hop (eight counts).

5 – 8   Repeat bars 1 – 4.

Source: W F Gillies Manual of Dancing or A Complete Companion to the Ballroom, Glasgow, c. 1885 and RSCDS Book 2.

Hamilton House

Sets of four couples in longwise formation. After one turn through the dance, the dancing couple finish in second place and repeat the dance from this position, dancing with the two couples below them and finish at the bottom of the set. After two turns, the new top couple begins.

Music: 8 x 32 bar jig

Two counts per bar

Tune: Colonel Hamilton's Delight.

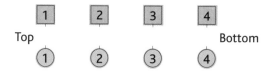

Bars

1 – 4   First woman advancing, sets to second man, and, giving both hands, turns third man to finish between second and third men.

5 – 8   First man advancing, sets to second woman and, giving both hands, turns third woman to finish between third couple, facing up.

On bars 7 – 8, first woman moves to be between second couple, who step up and face down.

9 – 12   First, second, and third couples set to partners twice.

13 – 16   First couple, giving both hands, turn each other to finish in second place on opposite sides. (This can also be a swing turn, pivot, or birl; dancers must ensure that they finish at the correct time and in the correct position.)

17 – 20   Second, first, and third couples set to partners twice.

21 – 24   First couple, giving both hands, turn each other halfway round to finish in second place on own sides.

25 – 32   Second, first, and third couples dance six hands round and back.

Repeat, having passed a couple.

Source: William Campbell's Fourth Collection of Country Dances and Cotillions 1790 and RSCDS Book 1.

The Highland Fair

Sets of four couples in longwise formation. After one turn through the dance, the dancing couple finish in second place, repeat the dance from this position, dancing with the couple below them, and finish in third place. For the third turn of the dance, the original dancing couple repeat with the couple below them and a new top couple begins.

Music: 8 x 32 bar jig

Two counts per bar

Tune: Muirland Willie.

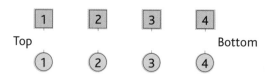

Bars

1 – 8   First couple cast off, dance behind own lines, turn away from partner and dance up to original places.

9 – 12   First and second couples, giving right hands, turn partners once round.

13 – 16	First and second couples, giving left hands, turn partners once round.
17 – 20	First couple, followed by second couple, who dance up the sides to begin, lead down the middle.
21 – 24	Second couple, followed by first couple, lead up to finish, second couple in first place and first couple in second place.
25 – 32	Second and first couples dance rights and lefts.

Repeat, having passed a couple.

Source: The Lady's Companion or Complete Pocket book for the year 1801 and RSCDS Graded Book.

Hooper's Jig

Sets of four couples in longwise formation. After one turn through the dance, the dancing couple finish in second place and repeat the dance from this position, dancing with the two couples below them and finish at the bottom of the set. After two turns, the new top couple begins.

Music: 8 x 32 bar jig

Four counts per bar

Tune: Peter's Peerie Boat.

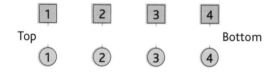

Top   Bottom

Bars

1 – 4   All clap as first couple, passing right shoulder, cross over, and cast off one place on opposite sides. Second couple step up on bars 3 – 4.

5 – 8   First and third couples dance right hands across once round.

9 – 12   All clap as first couple, passing right shoulder, cross over and cast up to original

places. Second couple step down on bars 11 – 12.

13 – 16   First and second couples dance left hands across once round.

17 – 18   First man and third woman, giving right hands, change places.

19 – 20   First woman and third man, giving right hands, change places. At the same time, first man and third woman continue to dance round each other's position, ready to cross back.

21 – 22   First man and third woman, giving right hands, change places and first man faces out. At the same time, first woman and third man continue to dance round each other's position, ready to cross back.

23 – 24   First woman and third man, giving left hands, cross over, with third man guiding first woman into second place, while first man casts off to second place. Second couple step up.

25 – 32   Second and first couples dance rights and lefts.

Repeat, having passed a couple.

Source: Traditional and Miss Milligan's Miscellany.

J B Milne

Sets of four couples in longwise formation. After one turn through the dance, the dancing couple finish in second place and repeat the dance from this position, dancing with the two couples below them, and finish at the bottom of the set. After two turns, the new top couple begin.

Music: 8 x 32 bar reel

Two counts per bar

| 1 | 2 | 3 | 4 |

Top   Bottom

Tune: J B Milne.

(1)   (2)   (3)   (4)

Bars

1 – 4   First man and second woman set advancing and, giving right hands, turn once round.

5 – 8   First woman and second man repeat.

9 – 16   First couple set advancing and, giving both hands, turn once round to finish facing the top. First couple cast off one place and dance a petronella turn to finish first woman between second couple, all facing down and first man between third couple, all facing up.

17 – 20   First couple set and, giving right hands, turn three-quarters to finish in second place

on opposite sides. At the same time, second and third women and second and third men, giving right hands, change places and set.

21 – 24 First couple set and, giving right hands, turn three-quarters to finish first woman between the couple in third place and first man between the couple in top place. At the same time, third and second couples, giving right hands, cross over and set.

25 – 28 First couple set and, giving right hands, change places. At the same time, third and second women and third and second men, giving right hands, change places and set.

29 – 30 First woman casts off to second place and first man casts up to second place. At the same time, second and third couples, giving right hands, cross over.

31 – 32 Second, first, and third couples set.

Repeat, having passed a couple.

Source: Hugh Foss and Collins Pocket Reference guide to Scottish Country Dancing (1996)

La Russe

Square set for four couples. The dance is repeated with second, third, and fourth couples leading in turn.

Music: 4 x 64 bar reel

Two counts per bar

Tune: La Russe.

Bars

1 – 2   All change places with partner, passing by the left, to face the dancer in partners' corner position. (Fig. 1)

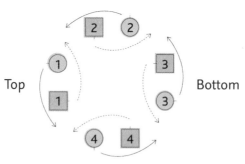

3 – 4   All set.

5 – 8	All turn the person in partners' corner position with both hands to finish facing own partners. (This can also be a swing turn, pivot, or birl.)
9 – 16	All set twice to partners and, giving both hands, turn one and a half times to finish in original places. (This can also be a swing turn, pivot, or birl.)
17 – 24	First man leads his partner in promenade hold anticlockwise round the inside of the set. They greet each couple as they pass.
25 – 32	First couple poussette round inside the set, to finish in original places.
33 – 40	First and third couples dance across to change places, first couple dancing between third couple. They dance back, third couple dancing between first couple.
41 – 48	First and third couples repeat bars 33 – 40.
49 – 56	All dance eight hands once round to the left.

57 – 64   The men give nearer hand to partners and, with the women joining right hands across, all dance once round to finish in original places.

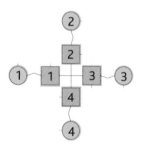

The dance is repeated with second, third, and fourth couples leading in turn.

There are many local variations to this dance that may be encountered; all versions are equally correct!

Source: Collected locally in Forfar and Miss Milligan's Miscellany.

La Tempête (The Tempest)

The couples stand in groups of four couples, two couples facing two couples, each man with his partner on his right.

Music: 8 x 48-bar reel

Two counts per bar

Tune: La Tempête.

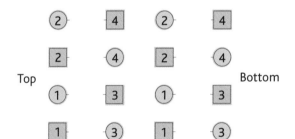

Bars

1 – 8   First and fourth couples dance right hands across and left hands back to places.

9 – 16   Second and third couples repeat bars 1 – 8.

17 – 24   First, second, third, and fourth couples set
twice to partners and, giving both hands,
turn once round. (This can also be a swing
turn, pivot, or birl; dancers must ensure that
they finish at the correct time and in the
correct position.)

25 – 28   First, second, third, and fourth couples with
both hands joined dance eight slip steps
(gallop) across to change places with
opposite couple, i.e. first with third and
second with fourth, the men passing back
to back.

29 – 32   First, second, third, and fourth couples
repeat bars 25 – 28 back to places, the
women passing back to back.

33 – 36   First and third couples and, at the same
time, second and fourth couples dance four
hands once round to the left.

37 – 40   First and third couples and, at the same
time, second and fourth couples, dance left
hands across back to places.

41 – 43   First, second, third, and fourth couples
advance two steps and retire one step.

44	First, second, third, and fourth couples clap three times.
45 – 48	First and second couples dancing down, pass under the raised arms of third and fourth couples, who have taken nearer hands to dance up.

First and second couples repeat bars 1 – 48 with the next two couples, and dance the same figures with every line until they arrive at the bottom of the room. As each line reaches the top or bottom of the room, dancers change to correct side of partners and stand during one turn of the dance.

Source: Collected locally and RSCDS Book 2.

The Machine without Horses

Sets of four couples in longwise formation. After one turn through the dance, the dancing couple finish in second place and repeat the dance from this position, dancing with the two couples below them and finish at the bottom of the set. After two turns, the new top couple begins.

Music: 8 x 32 bar jig

Two counts per bar

Tune: The Machine without Horses.

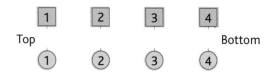

Bars

1 – 4   First couple set and cast off one place. Second couple step up on bars 3 – 4.

5 – 8   First and third couples dance right hands across once round.

9 – 12   First couple set and cast up one place. Second couple step down on bars 11 – 12.

13 – 16   First and second couples dance left hands across once round.

17 – 24   First couple, followed by second couple, who dance up the sides to begin, dance down between third couple, cast up round them, dance up to the top, and cast off into second place, and second couple dance up to top place.

25 – 32   Second and first couples dance rights and lefts.

Repeat, having passed a couple.

Source: Rutherford's Complete Collection of 200 of the most Celebrated Country Dances, 1775 and RSCDS Book 12.

Mairi's Wedding

Sets of four couples in longwise formation. After one turn through the dance, the dancing couple finish in second place and repeat the dance from this position, dancing with the two couples below them and finish at the bottom of the set. After two turns, the new top couple begins.

Music: 8 x 40 bar reel

Two counts per bar

Tune: Mairi's Wedding, also known as The Lewis Bridal Song

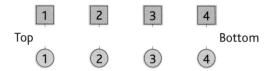

Bars

1 – 4   First couple, giving right hands, turn once round and cast off one place. Second couple step up on bars 3 – 4.

5 – 8	First couple, giving left hands, turn one and a quarter times to face first corners.
9 – 12	First couple dance a half reel of four with first corners, passing left shoulder in the middle to face second corners. (Note)
13 – 16	First couple dance a half reel of four with second corners, passing left shoulder in the middle to face first corners (who are in diagonally opposite position).
17 – 20	First couple dance a half reel of four with first corners, passing left shoulder in the middle to face second corners (who are in diagonally opposite position).
21 – 24	First couple dance a half reel of four with second corners to finish in second place on own sides.
25 – 32	First woman dances a reel of three across the dance, passing second man left shoulder to begin. At the same time, first man dances a reel of three across the dance with third couple, passing third woman left shoulder to begin. First couple finish in second place on own sides.

33 – 40	Second, first, and third couples dance six hands round and back.

Repeat, having passed a couple.

Note: In this dance it is common for first couple to pass right shoulders in the middle at the end of each of the half diagonal reels of four.

Source: James B Cosh and Collins Pocket Reference guide to Scottish Country Dancing (1996).

The Marquis of Lorne

Sets of four couples in longwise formation. After one turn through the dance, the dancing couple finish in second place and repeat the dance from this position, dancing with the two couples below them, and finish at the bottom of the set. After two turns, the new top couple begins.

Music: 8 x 32 bar strathspey

Four counts per bar

Tune: Marquis of Lorn's Strathspey.

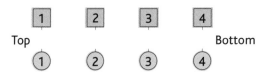

Bars

1 – 4   First couple, followed by second couple, who dance up the sides to begin, lead down the middle.

5 – 8   Second couple, followed by first couple, lead up to finish second couple in first place and first couple in second place.

9 – 16	Second, first, and third couples dance six hands round and back to finish with second couple facing each other, first couple facing down and third couple facing up.
17 – 24	Second, first, and third couples dance a grand chain.
25 – 32	First couple set twice and dance down between third couple, divide and cast up to second place.

Repeat, having passed a couple.

Source Miss Milligan's Miscellany.

Maxwell's Rant

Sets of four couples in longwise formation. After one turn through the dance, the dancing couple finish in second place and repeat the dance from this position, dancing with the two couples below them, and finish at the bottom of the set. After two turns, the new top couple begins.

Music: 8 x 32 bar reel

Two counts per bar

Tune: Maxwell's Rant.

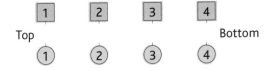

Bars

1 – 8   First couple, with second and third couples, dance reels of three on opposite sides of the set. First couple begin by crossing down, second couple dance out and up, and third couple dance in and up. First couple finish in partner place.

183

9 – 16   First couple, with second and third couples,
          dance reels of three on own sides of the set.
          First couple begin by crossing down, second
          couple dance out and up and third couple
          dance in and up. First couple finish in
          original place.

17 – 20   First couple, giving right hands, cross over
          and cast off one place. Second couple step
          up on bars 19 – 20.

21 – 24   First couple dance a half figure of eight
          round second couple.

25 – 28   First couple dance down between third
          couple and cast up to second place on own
          sides.

29 – 32   Second, first, and third couples, giving right
          hands, turn once round.

          Repeat, having passed a couple.

Source: Rutherford's Complete Collection of 200 of
the Most Celebrated Country Dances, 1756 and
RSCDS Book 18.

The Montgomeries' Rant

Sets of four couples in longwise formation. After one turn through the dance, the dancing couple finish in second place and repeat the dance from this position, dancing with the two couples below them and finish at the bottom of the set. After two turns, the new top couple begins.

Music: 8 x 32 bar reel

Two counts per bar

Tune: Lady Montgomerie.

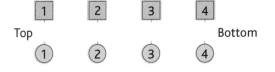

Bars

1 – 4   First couple, giving right hands, cross over and cast off one place on opposite sides.

5 – 8   First couple, giving left hands, cross over and first woman casts up one place while first man casts off one place. First woman finishes between second couple facing

second man, and first man between third couple facing third woman. Second couple step up on bars 3 – 4.

9 – 16   First woman with second couple and first man with third couple dance reels of three across the set. First woman and second man and first man and third woman passing right shoulder to begin. On bar 16, first couple, with nearer hands joined, face second woman.

Top

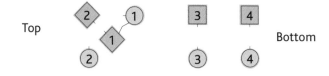

Bottom

17 – 24   First couple set to second woman. First couple turn towards each other and change hands to face third man and set. First couple move (veer) round to face third woman and set. First couple turn towards each other and change hands to face second man and set. First couple finish facing second corners.

25 – 30	Second, first, and third couples dance reels of three on the sides. First couple pass second corners right shoulder to begin.
31 – 32	First couple, giving right hands, cross to second place on own sides.
	Repeat, having passed a couple.

Source: Castle Menzies Manuscript (1749) and RSCDS Book 10.

Monymusk

Sets of four couples in longwise formation. After one turn through the dance, the dancing couple finish in second place and repeat the dance from this position, dancing with the two couples below them, and finish at the bottom of the set. After two turns, the new top couple begins.

Music: 8 x 32 bar strathspey

Four counts per bar

Tune: Monymusk.

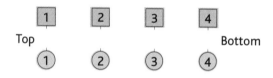

Bars

1 – 4   First couple, giving right hands, turn once round and cast off one place on own sides. Second couple step up on bars 3 – 4.

5 – 8   First couple, giving left hands, turn one and a quarter times to finish first woman between the second couple, facing down,

188

and first man between the third couple, facing up.

9 – 12   First woman with second couple and first man with third couple set twice. On bars 11 – 12, first couple dance to the right into second place on opposite sides of the set, pulling right shoulder back.

13 – 16   Second, first, and third couples set twice.

17 – 24   Second, first, and third couples dance six hands round and back.

25 – 30   Second, first, and third couples dance reels of three on the sides. First woman passes third man and first man passes second woman by the right shoulder to begin.

31 – 32   First couple, giving right hands, cross over to second place, on own sides.

Repeat, having passed a couple.

Source: Preston Twenty-four Country Dances for the Year 1786 and RSCDS Book 11.

Mrs MacLeod

Sets of four couples in longwise formation. After one turn through the dance, the dancing couple finish in second place and repeat the dance from this position, dancing with the two couples below them, and finish at the bottom of the set. After two turns, the new top couple begins.

Music: 8 x 32 bar reel

Two counts per bar

Tune: Mrs MacLeod of Raasay.

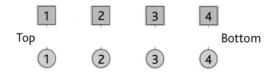

Bars

1 – 8   First and second couples dance right hands across and left hands back.

9 – 16   First couple lead down the middle and up to finish facing first corners. Second couple step up on bars 11 – 12.

17 – 20	First couple set to and turn first corners to finish in the middle, facing second corners.
21 – 24	First couple set to and turn second corners to finish in second place, on opposite sides, facing first corners.
25 – 30	Second, first, and third couples dance reels of three on the sides. First couple passing first corners left shoulder to begin.
31 – 32	First couple, giving right hands, cross over to second place on own sides.
	Repeat, having passed a couple.

Source: The Ballroom or the Juvenile Pupil's Assistant (1827) and RSCDS Book 6.

Petronella

Sets of four couples in longwise formation. After one turn through the dance, the dancing couple finish in second place, repeat the dance from this position, dancing with the couple below them, and finish in third place. For the third turn of the dance, the original dancing couple repeat with the couple below them and a new top couple begins.

Music: 8 x 32 bar reel

Two counts per bar

Tune: Petronella.

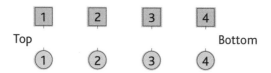

Bars

1 – 2   First couple dance a petronella turn (dance a three-quarters turn, moving diagonally to the right and pulling right shoulder back to face partner). See Petronella turn in Section 3.

3 – 4	First couple set to each other.
5 – 8	First couple repeat bars 1 – 4, always moving diagonally to the right, to finish in partner's place.
9 – 16	First couple repeat bars 1 – 8 to finish in original positions.
17 – 24	First couple lead down the middle and up to finish facing each other in the middle of the set with both hands joined. Second couple step in.
25 – 32	First and second couples dance a poussette.

Repeat, having passed a couple.

Source: The Ballroom or the Juvenile Pupil's Assistant (1827) and RSCDS Book 1.

The Provost Wynd

Sets of four couples in longwise formation. After one
turn through the dance, the dancing couple finish in
second place and repeat the dance from this position,
dancing with the two couples below them, and finish
at the bottom of the set. After two turns, the new top
couple begins.

Music: 8 x 32 bar reel

Two counts per bar

Tune: Ray's Reel.

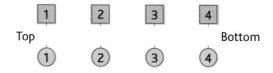

Bars

1 – 8   First, second, and third couples dance reels
of three on own sides. First and second men
and first and second women pass right
shoulder to begin.

9 – 12   First man and second woman, giving right
hands, turn once round.

13 – 16	First woman and second man, giving right hands, turn once round.
17 – 24	First couple, giving right hands, cross over, cast off two places, and, giving left hands, cross over and cast up one place. Second couple step up on bars 19 – 20.
25 – 28	First and third couples dance right hands across.
25 – 32	Second and first couples dance left hands across.
	Repeat, having passed a couple.

Source: RSCDS Graded Book 2.

The Reel of the 51st Division

Sets of four couples in longwise formation. After one turn through the dance, the dancing couple finish in second place and repeat the dance from this position, dancing with the two couples below them, and finish at the bottom of the set. After two turns, the new top couple begins.

Music: 8 x 32 bar reel

Two counts per bar

Tune: The Drunken Piper.

Bars

1 – 8   First couple set to each other and cast off two places, meet below third couple, and lead up the middle to face first corners. Second couple step up on bars 3 – 4.

9 – 12   First couple set to and turn first corners with the right hand, finishing in a diagonal line by joining left hands with partner.

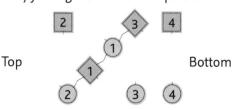

13 – 14	First couple and first corners balance in line (set).
15 – 16	First couple, releasing right hands with corners, turn each other one and a quarter times to face second corners.
17 – 22	First couple repeat bars 9 – 14 with second corners.
23 – 24	First couple cross to second place on own sides.
25 – 32	Second, first, and third couples dance six hands round and back.
	Repeat, having passed a couple.

Source: This dance was devised by members of the 51st Highland Division when they were POWs during WW2. The dance depicts a Saint Andrew's Cross formation which was intended to symbolise Scotland and the Highland Division. The dance was published in 1945 by the RSCDS in Book 13. The full story of the writing of this dance is fascinating and further details can be found on line at:

http://www.historyinanhour.com/2014/06/04/history-reel-51st-division/

The Reel of the Royal Scots

Sets of four couples in longwise formation. After one turn through the dance, the dancing couple finish in second place and repeat the dance from this position, dancing with the two couples below them, and finish at the bottom of the set. After two turns, the new top couple begins.

Music: 8 x 32 bar reel

Two counts per bar

Tune: The Reel of the Royal Scots.

Bars

1 – 2 First and second women, giving left hands, and first and second men, giving right hands, turn halfway to finish first couple back to back in the middle of the set at second place, and second couple in first place. First and third women join right hands and first and third men join left hands.

3 – 4 Second, first, and third couples set as in double triangles. (Fig.)

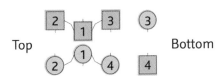

Top   Bottom

5 – 6   First and third women, retaining right hands, and first and third men, retaining left hands, turn halfway to finish third couple back to back in the middle of the set, and first couple in third place. Second and third women join left hands and second and third men join right hands.

7 – 8   Second, third, and first couples set as in double triangles.

9 – 16   First couple, followed by third couple, dance up between second couple to the top, cast off one place, and dance down the middle to third place. First couple cast up to second place and third couple dance into original places.

17 – 24   First couple, passing left shoulder, turn first corner with the right hand, pass partner right shoulder in the middle, turn second

corner with the right hand and, passing partner right shoulder, cross over to second place on own sides. Corners dance for four bars.

25 – 32 Second, first, and third couples dance six hands round and back.

Repeat, having passed a couple.

Source: Devised by Roy Goldring to celebrate the 350th Anniversary of the Royal Scots (The Royal Regiment) in 1983 and published by the RSCDS as a leaflet dance.

Shiftin' Bobbins

Sets of four couples in longwise formation. After one turn through the dance, the dancing couple finish in second place and repeat the dance from this position, dancing with the two couples below them and finish at the bottom of the set. After two turns, the new top couple begins.

Music: 8 x 32 bar reel

Two counts per bar

Tune: Shiftin' Bobbins.

Bars

1 – 2   First couple, giving right hands, cross down to finish back to back facing opposite sides. Second couple step up.

3 – 4   Joining nearer hands, all set. (Fig.)

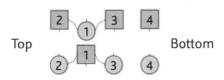

Top   Bottom

5 – 8	First couple cast up one place, meet, and dance down to second place (in the middle of the set).
9 – 12	First woman with second and third men dance right hands across once round, while first man with second and third women dance left hands cross once round.
13 – 16	First couple, followed by second and third couples, dance down the middle. All turn inwards to face up.
17 – 20	Third couple, followed by second and first couples, dance up. Third couple cast off to original place, second couple dance up to the top, and first couple finish in the middle of second place.
21 – 24	First woman with second and third men dance left hands across, while first man with second and third women dance right hands across.
25 – 28	First couple dance up and cast off to second place on opposite sides.

29 – 32 First couple dance a half figure of eight up round second couple to finish on own sides.

Repeat, having passed a couple.

Source: Roy Clowes and Collins Pocket Reference guide to Scottish Country Dancing (1996).

Speed the Plough *or* Inverness Country Dance

Sets of four couples in longwise formation. After one turn through the dance, the dancing couple finish in second place and repeat the dance from this position, dancing with the two couples below them, and finish at the bottom of the set. After two turns, the new top couple begins.

Music: 8 x 32 bar reel

Two counts per bar

Tune: Speed the Plough.

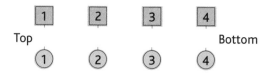

Bars

1 – 8   First and second couples dance right hands across and left hands back to places.

9 – 16	First couple lead down the middle and up to finish facing first corners. Second couple step up on bars 11 – 12.
17 – 20	First couple set to and turn first corners to finish back to back in the middle, facing second corners.
21 – 24	First couple set to and turn second corners to finish facing each other up and down these, with first woman between second couple at the top, and first man between third couple.
25 – 32	First couple set twice and, giving both hands, turn one and a quarter times to second place on own sides. (This can also be a swing turn; dancers must ensure that they finish at the correct time and in the correct position.)

Repeat, having passed a couple.

Source: Collected in Invernesshire and RSCDS Book 2.

The White Cockade

Sets of four couples in longwise formation. After one turn through the dance, the dancing couple finish in second place and repeat the dance from this position, dancing with the two couples below them, and finish at the bottom of the set. After two turns, the new top couple begins.

Music: 8 x 32 bar reel

Two counts per bar

Tune: The White Cockade.

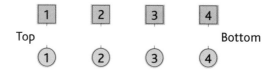

Bars

1 – 8   First, second, and third couples set and, giving right hands, cross over. Repeat back to places.

9 – 16   First couple lead down the middle and up to finish in first place in the middle of the set, facing up.

17 – 20   First couple cast off to second place on own sides. Second couple step up on bars 19 – 20.

21 – 24   First and third couples dance four hands once round to the left.

25 – 32   Second and first couples dance rights and lefts.

Repeat, having passed a couple.

Source: Preston Twenty-four Country Dances for the Year 1791 and RSCDS Book 5.

The White Heather Jig

Sets of four couples in longwise formation. After one turn through the dance, the dancing couple finish at the bottom of the set, and the new top couple begins.

Music: 4 x 40 bar jig

Two counts per bar

Tune: Six-Twenty Two Step.

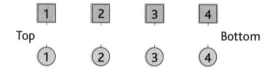

Bars

1 – 4   First couple, giving right hands, turn once round and cast off one place. Second couple step up on bars 3 – 4.

5 – 8   First couple, giving left hands, turn one and a half times to finish back to back between second couple, facing opposite sides.

9 – 16   First and second couples dance a reel of four across the dance, first couple finish facing first corners.

17 – 24   First couple turn first corners with the
          right hand, partner with the left hand,
          second corners with the right hand and
          partner with the left hand to finish back
          to back between third couple, facing
          opposite sides.

25 – 32   First and third couples dance a reel of
          four across the dance. Third couple finish
          in second place and first couple finish in
          the middle.

33 – 36   First couple, giving left hands, turn once
          round and cast off one place on own
          sides. Fourth couple step up on bars
          35 – 36.

37 – 40   First couple, giving right hand, turn
          once round (swing turn, pivot, or birl).

          Repeat with a new top couple.

Source: James B Cosh and Collins Pocket Reference
guide to Scottish Country Dancing (1996).

The Wild Geese

Sets of four couples in longwise formation. After one turn through the dance, the dancing couple finish in second place and repeat the dance from this position, dancing with the two couples below them and finish at the bottom of the set. After two turns, the new top couple begins.

Music: 8 x 32 bar jig

Two counts per bar

Tune: Mrs MacPherson of Cluny.

Bars

1 – 4   First and third couples set advancing to join nearer hands in a line up and down the set, men with partners on their right. First and third couples set.

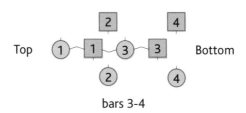

bars 3-4

5 – 8	First and third couples, retaining right hands with partner, turn three-quarters, then first couple cast off to third place on own sides, while third couple lead up to first place.
9 – 16	Third and first couples repeat bars 1 – 8, but on bars 15 – 16, third couple cast off while first couple lead up to original places.
17 – 24	First couple lead down the middle and up to second place on own sides. Second couple step up on bars 19 – 20.
25 – 32	Second and first couples dance rights and lefts.
	Repeat, having passed a couple.

Source: Collected by Jenny MacLachlan and published in RSCDS Book 24.

Appendix

Section 5 – Sources and devisers of dances:

The dances in this section have been previously published by the RSCDS.

Longwise Sets – 2 couple dances

The Duke of Atholl's Reel	RSCDS Book 16
The Highland Fair	RSCDS Graded Book
Petronella	RSCDS Book 1

Longwise Sets – 3 couple dances

The Birks of Invermay	RSCDS Book 16
The Deil amang the Tailors	RSCDS Book 14
Duke of Perth or Pease Strae or Broun's Reel	RSCDS Book 1
Flowers of Edinburgh	RSCDS Book 1
Hamilton House	RSCDS Book 7
Hooper's Jig	Miss Milligan's Miscellany

The White Cockade	RSCDS Book 5
The Wild Geese	RSCDS Book 24

Longwise Sets – 4 couple dances

Dunnet Head	Peter Knight (A Guide to SCD)
The White Heather Jig	James Cosh (A Guide to SCD)

Square Sets

La Russe	Miss Milligan's Miscellany
La Tempête (The Tempest)	RSCDS Book 2

Other Formations

Foursome Reel	RSCDS Book 3
The Glasgow Highlander	RSCDS Book 2

Photo credits

p17 & p24 Michael Greenwood, RSCDS

Index

Further information

Dance Scottish!

The Royal Scottish County Dance Society (RSCDS) is a Scottish Charity, with headquarters in Edinburgh and members throughout the world. Indeed, anywhere from Aberdeen to Adelaide, Munich to Moscow, Toronto to Tokyo you will find enthusiastic participants ready to dance reels, jigs and strathspeys to the wonderful tunes that are such an important part of Scotland's heritage.

The aim of the RSCDS is to build a vibrant, worldwide community of Scottish dancers and musicians of all ages and abilities.

The RSCDS, through its network of Branches and Affiliated Groups, provides support to its many dancers and teachers all over the globe. Currently there are 160 Branches and 310 Affiliated Groups. The RSCDS publishes regular magazines, newsletters, books of dances, books of music, resources for school teachers, and has a significant online presence. It also produces recorded music for a large number of dances, available on CD or as digital downloads.

There are many dance related events organised centrally, and even more organised by individual Branches or groups.

Those who wish to teach Scottish country dancing are well trained and supported. Although encouraging good standards of dancing, the RSCDS is keen to emphasise that dancing is a social pastime to be enjoyed by all, regardless of age or experience.For further information about the work of the RSCDS please contact:

The Royal Scottish Country Dance Society
12 Coates Crescent
Edinburgh
EH3 7AF

+44 (0)131 225 3854
info@rscds.org
www.rscds.org

Other useful links are:

http://www.strathspey.org

http://www.scottishdance.net

http://my.strathspey.org/dd/index/

https://www.scottish-country-dancing-dictionary.com

http://www.dufftowndanceclub.com/videos.html

http://www.scotland.org/features/ceilidh-dancing

Collins

LITTLE BOOKS

These beautifully presented Little Books make excellent pocket-sized guides, packed with hints and tips.

Bananagrams Secrets
978-0-00-825046-1
£6.99

Bridge Secrets
978-0-00-825047-8
£6.99

101 ways to win at Scrabble
978-0-00-758914-2
£6.99

Gin
978-0-00-825810-8
£6.99